Home Office

Custody, Care and Justice:
The Way Ahead for the Prison Service in England
and Wales

Presented to Parliament by
the Secretary of State for the Home Department
by Command of Her Majesty September 1991

Cm 1647   London: HMSO   £11.20 net

CONTENTS

The Home Secretary,
the Rt Hon Kenneth Baker MP

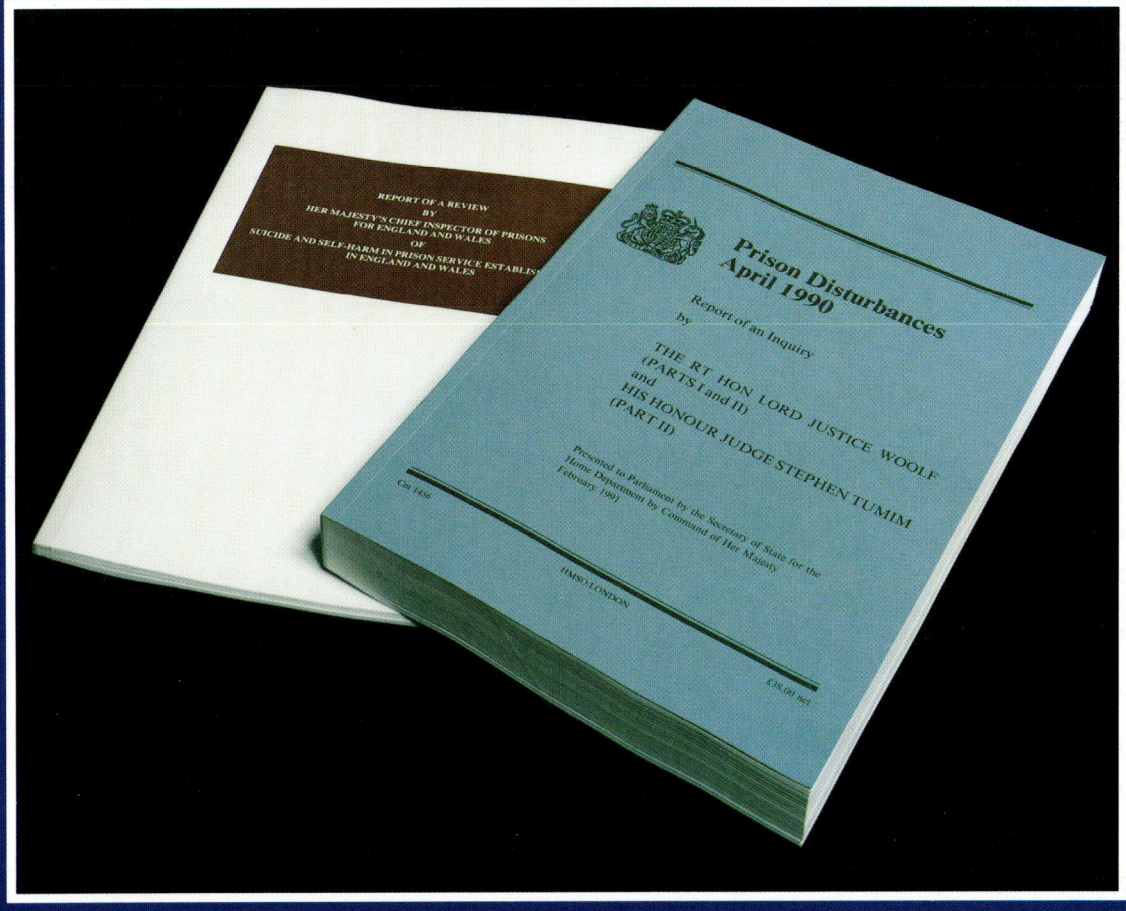

1 This White Paper charts a course for the Prison Service in England and Wales for the rest of this century and beyond.

2 The aim is to provide a better prison system. This will require more effective measures of security and control; a better and more constructive relationship between prisoners and staff; and more active, challenging and useful programmes for prisoners.

3 These requirements must be taken forward together in a balanced and co-ordinated way. Security must not be mistaken for repression. Constructive relationships must not engender laxity among staff. Active programmes must not lose sight of the nature of the prisoners with whom the Prison Service must deal or the public interest in preventing escapes or absconds. The necessary changes must be taken forward gradually over the coming years. Not everything can be implemented at once. Not everything can be afforded immediately.

4 Prisons must provide programmes for prisoners which keep them purposefully occupied during the working day. They must provide opportunities for education and training. They must do so in an environment which ensures that staff can maintain security and control, and in conditions which neither degrade prisoners nor demoralise staff.

5 Prisons which provide for prisoners in these ways are more likely to be stable and safe. They will be more likely to prevent escapes and reduce the risk and the consequences of serious disturbances. They are more likely to help prisoners prepare for release and to reduce the chance of sentenced prisoners offending again. Such prisons will be of value to prisoners, their families, the victims of serious crime and indeed to every citizen in this country. The Prison Service has an opportunity to play a greater part in helping to reduce crime. It must take it.

6 This represents for the Prison Service in England and Wales a challenge for change. It should be a challenge also to the prisoners in its care. The Prison Service is the agent which must secure the prisoner's custody. It must also be an agent for his or her change. No-one should underestimate the difficulty of the task. But it is a task which the Prison Service must tackle if it is to provide the service of which it is capable and which the public rightly requires.

7 The genesis of this White Paper was the report by Lord Justice Woolf and Judge Stephen Tumim on the prison disturbances in April 1990 (1). The disturbance at Manchester prison Strangeways which started on 1 April 1990 was the largest single disturbance in the history of the Prison Service in this country. It was followed by a series of disturbances at some 25 other prisons over the rest of the month. It was a traumatic and testing time for staff, prisoners and for the standing of the prison system. It put into relief some of the strengths of the Prison Service in which it can take pride. It demonstrated also weaknesses and inadequacies which must be remedied.

8 Lord Justice Woolf praised the members of the Prison Service as a whole for ensuring that the consequences of the disturbances were not still worse. But he found failures in the maintenance of control and in standards of justice. He noted that there could easily have been a collapse in security. The Woolf Report recognised that the Prison Service had embarked on a programme of change to make good past failures. But much still remained to be done to provide a Prison Service of which the country could be proud.

9 This White Paper sets out the Government's plans for a programme of change. The 12 key priorities are identified at the end of Chapter 1. The rest of the White Paper describes a challenging and far-reaching programme of change in accordance with these priorities. This is a programme designed to improve the quality of service provided by the Prison Service. It is a long term programme which will be worked on progressively over the coming years. It will influence the way the very considerable resources at present provided for the Prison Service are allocated. It will help identify the resources which are needed for the future. The provision of those resources will depend on the effectiveness with which the Prison Service makes use of its existing resources and on what the country can afford.

10 The Government has focused on three key areas of the Prison Service's work:

> **custody** – the first priority of any Prison Service is to keep in custody those committed to prison by the courts. That requires effective physical security measures and an alert and well-trained staff confident in their own safety and in the procedures to be followed when a security incident occurs. It requires a positive approach to security and control in prisons. It must be based on the quality of relationships between prisoners and staff and on providing prisoners with an active and worthwhile day in a secure environment located as near as possible to their home communities;

> **care** – staff have a responsibility not only for the custody but also for the care of prisoners. This must be reflected in staff training. It must be demonstrated through providing programmes and conditions for prisoners which treat them with humanity, dignity and respect;

> **justice** – prisoners should be required to exercise responsibility for what they do. They should be consulted and given explanations for decisions which affect them. The procedures for handling discipline and complaints must be effective and fair. Prisoners must be given opportunities to help them live law-abiding lives on release.

11 The Prison Service must improve its performance in all these areas. This is essential if the country is to have confidence in the prison system and if the Prison Service is to provide the best possible value for the resources invested in it. There should be no doubt that prisoners can and will be held securely and safely in prison establishments. Disorder of the kind seen in April 1990 cannot be tolerated or justified. Riots and disturbances on that scale must not happen again. Prisoners who present the greatest threat to the public cannot be permitted to escape. The Prison Service must prevent disruption and destruction. It must also positively and actively work towards helping prisoners make constructive use of their time in prison.

12 In setting its course for the Prison Service, the Government has taken careful account of the Report by Lord Justice Woolf and Judge Stephen Tumim on the Prison Disturbances in April 1990 (1). It has also considered carefully many other recent contributions, including the

Report by Judge Tumim, Her Majesty's Chief Inspector of Prisons, on Suicide and Self-harm in Prison Service Establishments in England and Wales (2), the Report on Prison Education by the House of Commons Education, Science and Arts Committee (3), and the Reports by the Chief Inspector of Prisons (4) and by Mr Lakes and Mr Hadfield (5) following the escape of two high risk Category A remand prisoners from Brixton prison on 7 July 1991.

13 The Woolf Report has made a considerable contribution to determining the Government's policy for the Prison Service. The Government accepts the central propositions in the Report that security and control must be kept in balance with justice and humanity and that each must be set at the right level. It has examined closely each of the 12 central recommendations in the Report and all of its 204 supporting proposals. The Woolf Report describes the recommendations as signposts setting the direction for the Prison Service in the years ahead. The Government has accepted the direction set by those recommendations. It has accepted the principal proposals which identify the route to follow. It is grateful to Lord Justice Woolf and Judge Tumim for preparing such a valuable and far-reaching report.

14 This White Paper recognises, as the Woolf Report recognised, that a better and more stable prison system requires a coherent and consistent strategy for the Prison Service. This White Paper provides such a strategy. It is the planned programme of change which the Woolf Report advocated: a programme which, as the Woolf Report proposed, looks at the picture as a whole. It is a strategy which derives from identifying the obligations of the Prison Service if it is to serve the public as an effective part of the criminal justice system in the 21st century. It looks to a Prison Service which is managed and run in a way which recognises and reflects those requirements. It identifies the work which the Prison Service has already undertaken to fulfil this role. It sets out clearly a programme of reform for the years ahead. Its purpose is to provide a Prison Service in England and Wales which serves the public and which looks after with humanity and justice all those in its care.

15 The Woolf Report drew carefully on submissions and public seminars from a wide range of individuals and organisations. This White Paper has benefited from that work. It reflects also discussions with Prison Service staff and prisoners, submissions from other organisations, and a range of seminars and discussions which have been held by organisations and groups since the Woolf Report was published.

16 The proposals in this White Paper also reflect the relevant principles for better public service identified in the Government's recent White Paper "The Citizen's Charter" (6). Prisoners remain citizens even though they have been charged with or convicted of committing an offence. Proposals of particular relevance include:

▶ the wearing of name badges by staff (Chapter 4);

▶ the preparation of a code of standards (Chapter 6);

▶ greater openness with prisoners (Chapter 7);

▶ new arrangements for handling prisoners' complaints and appeals against disciplinary findings (Chapter 8).

17   The programme of change set out in the following Chapters identifies a number of specific plans on which further consultations and discussions will be necessary. Anyone who wishes to comment on these or other matters is invited to write by 30 November 1991 to:

The Secretary to the Prisons Board
The Prison Service
Room 534
Cleland House
Page Street
LONDON
SW1P 4LN

Notes

(1) "Prison Disturbances April 1990", Report of an Inquiry by the Right Hon Lord Justice Woolf (Parts I & II) and His Honour Judge Stephen Tumim (Part II), HMSO, February 1991 (Cm 1456).

(2) "Report of a Review by Her Majesty's Chief Inspector of Prisons for England and Wales of Suicide and Self-harm in Prison Service Establishments in England and Wales", HMSO, December 1990 (Cm 1383).

(3) "Prison Education", Second Report of the House of Commons Education, Science and Arts Committee Session 1990-1991, HMSO, March 1991(HC 311 – I, II).

(4) "Inquiry by Her Majesty's Chief Inspector of Prisons into the escape of two Category A prisoners from Her Majesty's Prison Brixton on 7 July 1991", August 1991.

(5) "Interim report of a security audit of arrangements for holding and managing Category A prisoners in custody" by G H Lakes and R Hadfield, August 1991.

(6) "The Citizen's Charter", White Paper, HMSO, July 1991 (Cm 1599).

1 Prison Service
Statement of Purpose
– HMP Durham

2 Gatehouse –
HMP Birmingham

3 Officer and prisoner
on landing – HMP
Birmingham

4 Sentence plan discussion between prisoner, officer and probation officer – HMP Stocken

5 Race Relations Manual – launched April 1991

6 Young offenders' basketball – HMYOI Onley

4

5

6

The Prison Service as a Part of the Criminal Justice System

1.1   The Prison Service is a part of the criminal justice system. Imprisonment is the most serious power available to that system and it places heavy duties on those who administer it. This is recognised in the Prison Service's Statement of Purpose issued in 1988 which is on display in all Prison Service buildings. The statement is:

Home Office

HM PRISON SERVICE

"Her Majesty's Prison Service serves the public by keeping in custody those committed by the courts.

Our duty is to look after them with humanity and to help them lead law-abiding and useful lives in custody and after release."

1.2   The Prison Service's role needs to meet the changing requirements of the criminal justice system. It must be consistent with international human rights obligations. It must be responsive to changes in understanding of what imprisonment should be expected to achieve.

1.3   The primary purposes of a sentence of imprisonment are to punish the offender and to protect the public by depriving the offender of his or her liberty. The Prison Service's role is to keep the person in custody, to help him or her make constructive use of the time in prison and to help sentenced prisoners not to commit further crimes. That role is set out in the Statement of Purpose. It is a role which recognises the place of the Prison Service in today's criminal justice system. It permits the Service to make a distinctive contribution which complements the efforts of others in seeking to prevent crime. It requires it to do so in a way which recognises its duty as part of the criminal justice system to ensure that prisoners are treated with justice, humanity, dignity and respect.

1.4   The following sections of this Chapter consider ways for developing co-operation between the Prison Service and other parts of the criminal justice system; they clarify the role which the Prison Service should perform in the coming years; and they set out the Government's priorities for change.

Closer Co-operation

1.5   The Government's policies on crime are set out in its Green Paper "Punishment, Custody and the Community", published in July 1988 (1) and in the White Paper "Crime, Justice and Protecting the Public", published in February 1990 (2). Both identify reducing crime as the ultimate objective of Government policy and of the criminal justice system. This objective will not be achieved if those involved in it fail to co-operate and if there is no common understanding of the place of each in the system.

1.6   The provisions of the Criminal Justice Act 1991 bring this into high relief. The Act establishes that a custodial sentence should be used only to punish the most serious offences and to protect the public from violent and sexual offenders. The Act confirms the principle that a sentence of imprisonment does not end with release from prison: it continues under supervision in the community. There must be a continuum between life in prison and life in the community. To provide the best opportunity to prevent re-offending, what prisoners do in prison must be related to and lead into the arrangements for their supervision on release. This requires close co-operation and good understanding between the Prison and probation services.

1.7 As the Woolf Report recognised, it has been the Government's policy for some years to encourage greater co-operation within the criminal justice system. There are already a large number of initiatives which bring together those involved with varying degrees of formality. In addition to Ministerial meetings, there are regular trilateral meetings on criminal justice issues between senior officials of the Lord Chancellor's Department, the Home Office and the Crown Prosecution Service. There is also a developing pattern of regional and local liaison arrangements between the criminal justice services. Since 1989 the Home Office has organised a series of Special Conferences with the aim of promoting greater understanding and co-operation between participants in the criminal justice services.

1.8 These initiatives have shown that it is possible to develop useful co-operation in a wide variety of ways which do not encroach on the independence of the judges, Crown prosecutors, magistrates or the police. Similarly, any further consultative arrangements must be structured to ensure independence is preserved. Lord Justice Woolf and Judge Tumim were particularly well placed to reflect on these issues. The Woolf Report stressed that the national forum it recommended should not be a

Sentencing Council. The Government endorses that view.

1.9 The Government accepts the Woolf Report's recommendation that closer co-operation between the different parts of the criminal justice system is required. Such co-operation will enable those at or near the apex of the system to have a strategic view of the way the various parts relate to each other, and will help those with operational responsibilities to carry them out more effectively.

1.10 The Government has decided, therefore, to establish a national forum for the criminal justice system. It will be called the Criminal Justice Consultative Council, as the Woolf Report proposed. Its terms of reference will be:

To promote better understanding, co-operation and co-ordination in the administration of the criminal justice system; in particular by:

i) considering reports about developments in and affecting criminal justice;

ii) considering other information about the operation of the system; and

iii) overseeing the arrangements for Special Conferences;

but excluding consideration of individual cases.

1.11 The Council's members will be a senior judge, appointed by the Lord Chief Justice with the concurrence of the Lord Chancellor; representatives of Government Departments, including the Prison Service; the Crown

Prosecution Service; the magistracy and justices' clerks; and the police and probation services. Others will be co-opted as necessary, for example a representative of the Department of Health.

1.12 The Criminal Justice Consultative Council will be set up as soon as possible.

1.13 The Government agrees in principle that area committees should replace the present circuit liaison meetings. Since the police, probation service, magistrates' courts and the Crown Prosecution Service are all organised on the basis of counties, or combinations of counties, it should make for more effective co-operation between the services to establish the area committees on the same basis. Prison Service Area Managers would be closely involved and other services and organisations could be co-opted according to the topics which the committee was to discuss. These committees would keep under review the operation of the criminal justice system in the area and work to improve co-ordination between the services.

1.14 The Government will give further consideration to the role and composition of area committees and to their relationship with the arrangements for consultation which already exist on these lines in some areas. It will also consider any revisions necessary following the review of the structure of local government by the Local Government Commission which the Government intends to establish, subject to Parliament's approval of the necessary legislation.

The Role of the Prison Service

1.15 The country will continue to depend on sentences of imprisonment as part of the response to serious crime. There will continue to be those for whom imprisonment is the only practicable sentence of the court. It will continue to be in the public interest for courts to remand some people in custody awaiting trial or sentence.

1.16 But the effects of imprisonment can be severe. It breaks up families. It is hard for prisoners to retain or subsequently to secure law-abiding jobs. Imprisonment can lessen people's sense of responsibility for their actions and reduce their self-respect, both of which are fundamental to law abiding citizenship. Some, often the young and less experienced, acquire in prisons a wider knowledge of criminal activity. Imprisonment is costly for the individual, for the prisoner's family and for the community.

1.17 The Government has continued, therefore, to promote and make provision for community penalties and support for people on bail. The Criminal Justice Act 1991 takes forward this policy by introducing further provisions to ensure that sentences of imprisonment are used primarily for those who have committed the most serious offences, especially violent or sexual crimes.

1.18 The prison population is likely to change in nature and size over the coming years. Those remanded in custody will be those who cannot safely be held anywhere else, despite improvements in the provision in the community and a better flow of information to courts. With the introduction of unit fines, there should be fewer prisoners serving sentences for non-payment. There is likely to be a smaller proportion of prisoners serving shorter-term sentences for non-violent offences. There should be fewer mentally disordered prisoners awaiting transfer to a hospital under the provisions of the Mental Health Act.

1.19 As a result, the Prison Service will in future be dealing primarily with those who have committed or have been accused of committing the most serious offences. The population of adult prisoners with life sentences and young offenders with equivalent sentences has increased by an average of 120 a year since 1980. It is likely to continue to increase between now and the end of the century. There is likely to be a reduction in the numbers of young men under 30 serving prison sentences, and an increase in those aged over 30. Many will be hardened and experienced criminals. Some will be well used to manipulating and influencing people for their own ends, and in planning carefully their illegal activities. Others, however, will be inadequate people with poor educational achievements, bad or non-existent work records, and without the skills necessary to conduct social relationships in a co-operative and non-violent way.

1.20 In summary:

▶ imprisonment will remain a necessary option for the courts;

▶ the decisions of the courts are likely to lead to a population serving longer periods for more serious crimes, together with a substantial proportion of prisoners on remand;

▶ there will continue to be all manner and types of person in prison.

1.21 The Prison Service must meet the requirement of the courts to provide for these prisoners. This places three obligations on the Prison Service that are central to its role. They are that:

▷ the court's decision must be implemented;

▷ the regime must be positive;

▷ the prisoner must be prepared for release.

Implementing the Court's Decision

1.22 The court has decided that a person should lose his or her liberty by being held in custody. The first and overriding obligation of the Prison Service is to implement that decision. It follows from this that the Prison Service should keep the prisoner in custody; ensure the maintenance of order; assist the prisoner in dealing with the immediate consequences of imprisonment – both domestically and in preparing for any court hearing; provide the basic necessities of life; and expect sentenced prisoners to work to contribute to the cost of their upkeep.

1.23 The loss of liberty entails the loss of rights and freedom which others enjoy. But the loss of rights is not absolute. Under English law, a convicted prisoner retains all civil rights which are not taken away expressly or by necessary implication (3). An unconvicted prisoner on remand retains all rights other than those necessarily lost as a consequence of being held in custody.

Providing a Positive Regime

1.24 The deprivation of liberty can be a debilitating experience for a prisoner. The Prison Service has an obligation to help the prisoner make the best use of his or her time. There must be a positive regime to prevent prisoners falling into lethargy and despair. The Prison Service must concentrate particularly on young offenders, on those it receives in prison for the first time and on those who might be at risk of committing suicide or of harming themselves.

1.25 By their nature prisons necessarily restrict freedom of choice and many of the pleasures and opportunities of everyday life. Prisoners can became embittered and resentful. They need to be sustained – physically, mentally, emotionally, spiritually and socially.

1.26 In all these areas, the Prison Service has an obligation to do everything it can, consistent with maintaining a person's loss of liberty, to help make imprisonment a positive and constructive experience. It can do so through the programmes and facilities it provides and in the way it treats prisoners. It can look for opportunities to introduce a breath of normal life into prisons. It should have concern for all those in its care.

Preparing for Release

1.27 The third obligation is to prepare a prisoner for release. This applies to both remand and sentenced prisoners. For the former, the objective is to ensure that they can pick up the threads of their lives which were broken by the order of the court. For the latter, there is the additional objective of seeking to help them not to reoffend.

1.28 Offenders are not given sentences of imprisonment by the courts for the purpose of ensuring their rehabilitation. Most offenders are usually likely to have a better prospect of reform if they stay in the community. But if a court decides that an offender has to be sentenced to imprisonment, then the Prison Service has a duty to do everything in its power

to help that prisoner lead a law-abiding life after release.

What Prisons Should Provide

1.29 The three obligations of the Prison Service have been set out in their order of priority, and indeed of ascending difficulty. These obligations must be met if the Prison Service is to provide an effective service. They will require a prison system which provides in all establishments:

▷   **secure prisons.** The Prison Service must be able to hold all those likely to be committed to prison in the degree of security necessary to prevent their escape. Prisoners should not be held in conditions of security higher or lower than are necessary to achieve this objective. Security and order are most likely to be achieved by the provision of a constructive and active day for prisoners and maintained through the alertness and well-rehearsed skills of staff backed by well-designed physical security measures;

▷   **stable prisons.** The quality of the relationship between prisoners and staff is the key to a stable prison system. The right relations can be achieved only if the Service is managed at all levels in a way which enables such relationships to be sustained. Stable prisons require a mature relationship between staff and prisoners which ensures that both prisoners and staff are treated, and treat each other, as individuals, with dignity and with respect; and which encourages prisoners to make responsible choices and so retain and, if possible, enhance their confidence and self-respect;

▷ **safe prisons.** Prisoners and staff must feel that they and their possessions are safe. An atmosphere of insecurity, oppressiveness, and threat is not conducive to establishing constructive relationships. Fear is not a foundation on which to build respect or human dignity. The design and management of prisons must be directed to providing a safe environment which is not oppressive;

▷ **just prisons.** The necessary loss of many rights of citizenship need not normally prevent prisoners from knowing clearly what is expected of them; from having some choice over and being consulted about changes to their lives in prison; from knowing what will be provided in the establishment in which they are accommodated; from being given the reasons for decisions which affect them; from having a fair and just system for disciplinary hearings and for resolving grievances; and from being given facilities and programmes which reflect their legal status;

▷ **caring prisons.** The Prison Service must be ready to assist prisoners in dealing with the problems which follow on from the loss of their liberty. It can do so by staff being ready to offer ordinary human support, by specialised counselling, by the quality of its health care, by creating links with outside agencies – both statutory and voluntary – and by enabling prisoners to maintain contact with the outside world;

▷ **decent prisons.** Prison establishments should offer living conditions which recognise the Prison Service's

responsibility for the prisoner's environment for 24 hours a day. Questions of luxury or comfort are not the point at issue. Conditions should be set at the level which meets the Prison Service's obligations;

▷ **productive prisons.** Convicted prisoners should be required to work. It is a useful discipline in itself and in preparing prisoners for release. They should work on maintaining the environment of the prison and of the prison estate. They should be engaged in productive and challenging work in workshops and in farms and gardens. They may be given opportunities to contribute to charitable causes;

▷ **positive prisons.** The prisoner's time should be planned, in consultation with him or her, in a way which provides the opportunity where necessary for the individual to face up to what he or she has done and work towards ways of avoiding crime in future; to increase social and physical skills and educational competence; and to make realistic preparations for release. Prisons should provide every opportunity practicable for prisoners to maintain links with home. Prisoners should be given opportunities for achieving something in prison which they can take forward following their release.

1.30 Prisons are about people: the sort of prisons which are required depend on providing the physical security and conditions necessary to create an environment in which constructive relations between prisoners and staff can be established. The Prison Service must look after prisoners in accordance with these standards if it is to serve the public and help to prevent crime.

Priorities

1.31 This represents a considerable challenge for change.

1.32 The Woolf Report recognises the programme of change which the Prison Service has pursued in recent years. It has been a programme backed by substantial financial resources. The Government wishes to see that programme continue. It should be a programme which is practical, affordable, and which will, over the coming years, produce the changes which are necessary to provide a quality of service in which the country can have confidence and pride.

1.33 Better prisons cannot be achieved through a piecemeal approach. The changes required are inter-dependent. There needs, for example, to be a stable and secure environment for prisoners and staff if active and positive programmes are to be provided. Such programmes can only be effective if staff are trained and deployed to this work and know that they have the support and confidence of management in what they do. The delivery of these regimes should reduce tension and avoid a counter-productive concentration on physical and staff-intensive security measures. The programmes should be co-ordinated with what may be available to the prisoner from other agencies after release. Such programmes will not reach their full potential unless they are taken forward with the understanding of and assistance from other parts of the criminal justice system.

1.34 The Prison Service must have clear priorities in carrying out its programme of change in the years ahead. The Government considers that the priorities should be:

▶ to improve necessary security measures;

▶ to improve co-operation with other services and institutions, by working closely with the probation service and by membership of a national forum and area committees;

▶ to increase delegation of responsibility and accountability to all levels; with clear leadership and a published annual statement of objectives;

▶ to improve the quality of jobs for staff;

▶ to recognise the status and particular requirements of unconvicted prisoners;

▶ to provide active and relevant programmes for all prisoners, including unconvicted prisoners;

▶ to provide a code of standards for conditions and activities in prisons which will be used to set improvement targets in the annual contracts made between prison Governors and their Area Managers;

▶ to improve relationships with prisoners, including a statement of facilities for each prisoner, sentence plans, consultations, reasons for decisions and access to an independent appeal body for grievances and disciplinary decisions;

▶ to provide access to sanitation at all times for all prisoners;

▶   to end overcrowding;

▶   to divide the larger wings in prisons into smaller, more manageable units wherever possible;

▶   to develop community prisons which will involve the gradual realignment of the prison estate into geographically coherent groups serving most prisoners within that area.

1.35   These priorities establish a specific and clear programme for the Prison Service in the years ahead. They follow closely on the Woolf Report's recommendations. They are the main pointers to which other actions will be related. These actions, together with the key priorities, are described in the Chapters which follow. They will, as the Woolf Report recognises, take some years to realise. They are interrelated and inter-dependent. They reflect a coherent penal policy which recognises that it will continue to be necessary to deprive some people of their liberty when no other course is possible; and which recognises the consequences for the work of the Prison Service flowing from that decision.

Notes

(1) "Punishment, Custody and the Community", Green Paper, HMSO, July 1988 (Cm 424).

(2) "Crime, Justice and Protecting the Public", White Paper, HMSO, February 1990 (Cm 965).

(3) *Raymond v. Honey* [1983] 1 A.C. 1.

1

2

1 Emergency control room – HMP Frankland

2 Control and restraint training – Prison Service College, Newbold Revel

3 Improvements to
roof security —
HMP Manchester
in May 1991

4 Modern security
design

Introduction

2.1 The first priority of the Prison Service is to hold and manage prisoners in such a way as to prevent escapes and absconds. It must achieve this in a manner which is consistent with the responsibility of any part of the criminal justice system to act humanely, fairly and with justice; and in a way which, wherever possible, contributes to the positive obligations on the Prison Service described in Chapter 1.

2.2 The Prison Service must also maintain control in its establishments. That is required of every well-ordered institution. It is a particular requirement for the Prison Service. Loss of control can lead to a breach in security. It spreads fear and loss of confidence among prisoners as well as staff. It is an unacceptable breach of civilised standards. Both prisoners and staff should feel safe in the prison environment. Order must prevail.

2.3 The maintenance of security and control is a fundamental skill in the management of prisons and prisoners. It is a skill which sets the Prison Service apart from most other organisations or professions involved in the management of institutions. Prisoners do not choose to go to prison and need to be held there against their will. Coercion and force must be available as last resorts when control and order are in jeopardy or have broken down. But the skill of the Prison Service lies in deploying a positive approach to security based on staff building up effective relationships with prisoners. These relationships can help in giving warning of security difficulties; they are essential in helping prisoners make positive and not destructive use of their time.

2.4 A secure and stable prison system must also provide opportunities for prisoners to come to terms with their sentences, or the reasons why the court has remanded them in custody. Daily routines must be seen as fair, reasonable, predictable and humane. There must be effective means for responding to complaints and grievances. Prisoners should be engaged in full and active programmes which are challenging, purposeful, and which can be seen by them as relevant to their time in prison, as well as engendering some hope for a more productive future. There should be positive and mature relationships between prisoners and staff. The programmes for prisoners discussed in Chapter 7 are intended to contribute to these objectives.

2.5 Disciplinary procedures are also a means of maintaining control in an establishment. A well-managed prison should not have to rely on the extensive exercise of disciplinary powers. But a prison system which commands the confidence and respect of prisoners and staff must have a clear framework for identifying and punishing unacceptable behaviour. That framework should be seen as fair and just. The procedures for disciplinary proceedings and for the consideration of prisoners' grievances are discussed in Chapter 8.

2.6 Physical security measures, and a staff alert to and trained in the procedures for restoring control are therefore only a part of providing effective security and control in an establishment. They are, however, essential if prisoners are not to escape and are to live in an environment in which they can feel secure. They are important in order to help staff feel secure and to enable them to relate confidently and sensitively to prisoners. An insecure prison is a frightened prison. Fear is no foundation on which to build productive programmes or good relationships.

Recent Developments

2.7 The Prison Service has sought to strengthen security and control in prisons in recent years. In particular:

▶ the up-grading of the physical security of establishments has formed a key part in the building refurbishment programme;

▶ new techniques for handling disruptive prisoners or groups of prisoners have been introduced. By March 1991 approximately 50% of officers in closed establishments had been trained in control and restraint techniques for handling individual prisoners with the least risk of injury to both parties. By November 1990, the Prison Service had met its target of training some 4,200 officers in the more advanced techniques necessary for responding to disturbances. Since that date, a further 500 officers have been trained. The Prison Service aims to maintain at this level the number of those trained in advanced techniques. Lord Justice Woolf, in his Report, noted that the Service was fortunate in having developed such effective techniques which compared favourably with those developed in other countries visited by the Inquiry;

▶ the incident management arrangements in headquarters have been reviewed and revised since April 1990. There are now better arrangements for any serious incident to be managed by one of three operational Directors. There is a new and enlarged incident control suite in headquarters with improved communications and facilities. Headquarters contingency plans have been tested. The new arrangements reflect the detailed proposals on headquarters incident management made in the Woolf Report;

▶ the roles of headquarters and the headquarters incident manager have been clarified since April 1990. Headquarters provides advice, support and resources to the Governor in charge of handling the incident at the establishment. Operational decisions are for that Governor, subject only to the headquarters incident manager withholding approval for the Governor's strategy and tactics. On major operational questions, this power of veto would normally only be exercised after consultation with Ministers.

Future Direction

2.8 The maintenance of good security and control requires regular up-dating and constant vigilance. The Prison Service will, therefore, introduce significant new measures in the management of security in prisons and in the preparation of contingency plans. Its aims in doing so are:

▷ to ensure that there is sufficient physical security to deter prisoners from causing disturbances and to prevent their escape;

▷ to isolate any incidents which occur and prevent them from spreading to other parts of the prison;

▷ to ensure that there is an effective and well-rehearsed response by prison management and staff to any incident which arises.

Security Measures

2.9 The Government is committed to providing the statutory powers necessary for the Prison Service to maintain security in its prisons. The Government has therefore announced its intention to introduce as soon as Parliamentary time permits a new offence of prison mutiny and to increase the maximum penalty for aiding and abetting a prison escape from five to ten years imprisonment. These measures will provide more effective responses to prisoners who present the most serious threats to security, good order and control.

2.10 The Prison Service will operate a series of consistent standards for the maintenance of security in prison. These relate to physical standards, to the checking of those standards, to the handling of intelligence and to the operation of procedures. In particular, the Prison Service will:

▶ **issue a new security manual in the next few weeks to all prison establishments.** The manual will establish a clear set of standards for the security required in an establishment and for the handling of intelligence. It will incorporate many of the specific proposals relating to security in the Woolf Report and in the findings following the escape from Brixton prison on 7 July 1991;

▶ **conduct security audits in all closed establishments at least annually,** starting in the autumn of this year. These audits will provide a basis for preparing action plans to remedy any security deficiencies which they identify;

▶ **review the security of roofs in closed prisons, the scope for providing in** existing prisons smaller living units protected by gates, and the scope for securing better the areas in prisons where prisoners congregate. Standards for the physical security of existing establishments have been drawn up as a basis for conducting this review. The standards provide for the incorporation of defendable barriers or "firebreaks" to prevent disturbances spreading, as proposed in the Woolf Report. The implementation of the reviews will form part of the Prison Service's long term building and refurbishment programme. The pace of implementation must avoid unacceptable disruption to establishments and to their capacity to hold prisoners;

▶ **continue to require Governors to consider carefully the circumstances in which prisoners are permitted to gather together,** taking account of the objectives of the occasion and the risks to security and control. The introduction of smaller units and more secure areas should help in the management of prisoners in the future;

▶ **review the procedures for prisoners to be temporarily released from prison without escorting officers,** taking account of the compassionate and other circumstances in which such releases are made, set against the risks of the prisoner absconding and the likely consequences;

▶ **install x-ray machines in all prisons holding Category A prisoners,** to assist in searching goods and materials brought into these establishments. These machines are being installed as quickly as possible;

▶ **extend the use of electric locks for gates providing access to living units and other areas of the prison, subject to the outcome of a trial project at Manchester prison.** Electric locks would be used to override manual locks when required, for example if a disturbance broke out. Electric override systems should make it unnecessary for there to be different keys for different units since prisoners who took an officer's keys in one unit could not use them to get out. These systems are preferable to staff having keys which gave them access only to a single unit – some staff work regularly on more than one unit and all staff must be able to help in an emergency. Subject to experience with the trial project, therefore, electric locks will be introduced as part of the Prison Service's continuing refurbishment programme. In the meantime, reviews will be conducted at each establishment to determine how best to reduce the risk which arises from the capture of staff keys;

▶ **issue a manual consolidating advice on physical security and control requirements for existing establishments.** This manual will be available to all those involved in planning the modification and refurbishment of prison buildings.

Contingency Planning

2.11 The Prison Service aims to produce a consistent standard of contingency planning in establishments, and to ensure that the plans are understood and well-rehearsed by all those involved. Following the escape from Brixton prison on 7 July 1991, all prison establishments were instructed to review their contingency plans to ensure that they specifically covered incidents involving firearms or explosives. For the future, the Prison Service will:

▶ **issue a new contingency planning manual to all prison establishments.** This will lay down standards for contingency planning for all establishments. It will provide guidelines and procedures for Governors to plan an effective response to a whole range of emergencies. It will take account of and reflect many of the specific proposals in the Woolf Report about the handling of incidents and the findings following the escape from Brixton prison on 7 July 1991;

▶ **instruct establishments to carry out regular exercises and test the arrangements in their contingency plans**, involving the police and emergency services as necessary.

Incident Response

2.12 The effectiveness of a prison's response to a particular incident will be assisted by the quality of its contingency plans and by the degree to which they are understood and followed by all involved. In addition, the Prison Service has:

▶ **identified a number of Governors at Governor 3 level as incident co-ordinators.** They will be provided with the training necessary to keep them up to date with developments in incident management. They will be able to be called from their establishment or from their post in headquarters to plan and manage any physical intervention necessary to bring to an end a serious incident in any establishment. They will act under the authority of the Governor of the establishment and report to him or her;

▶ **maintained links with the police and the other emergency services.** The aim has been to ensure that the respective roles of each service are clear and fully understood.

2.13 For the future, the Prison Service will:

▶ **improve the training of governor grades in commanding an incident.** A new specialist course has been provided at the Prison Service College and two have already been held. The Prison Service will supplement this course by one-day seminars and exercises for governor grades;

▶ **improve staff counselling after incidents.** Incidents may involve disturbances or other highly stressful events, such as a prisoner's suicide, a violent escape attempt or a member of staff taken hostage. In May 1991 a scheme was introduced for the care and support of all Prison Service staff involved in an incident, based on the formation at each prison of a multidisciplinary care team. A stress management training package has also been developed and is available in all establishments. It is intended that the majority of staff will have taken this training package in the course of the next year. The Prison Service is considering the case for a Prison Service Counselling Service to build on the work already done

by the Home Office Staff Welfare Service and the Civil Service Occupational Health Service;

▶ **explore with the emergency services the possibility of joint training** for responding to disturbances and other serious incidents;

▶ **extend training for members of Boards of Visitors in relation to the important role they undertake on behalf of prisoners and staff during an incident;**

▶ **following consultations, issue guidance on the appropriate scope of press briefings** given by trade union representatives and members of Boards of Visitors during an incident;

▶ **continue to refine and develop the equipment, methods and command arrangements for the use of control and restraint techniques in response to a serious incident.** This work will follow closely the relevant proposals in the Woolf Report.

Conclusion

2.14 The measures outlined in this Chapter have two principal objectives. First, they are to provide the security necessary within which the right relations and active and relevant programmes can be developed with prisoners. Secondly, they are to ensure that prison staff in establishments and at headquarters can respond quickly and effectively to any incident which may occur so that the risk of injury, damage and escape is minimised, and so that the Prison Service can continue to provide an effective service. Such measures are essential if the Prison Service is to fulfil its obligations properly and to do so in a way which maintains the confidence of staff and the security of prisoners.

1

2

1 *Meeting with the Home Secretary, the Rt Hon Kenneth Baker MP*

2 *Prisons Minister the Rt Hon Angela Rumbold CBE MP with staff – Prison Service College, Newbold Revel*

3 *The Prisons Board*

3

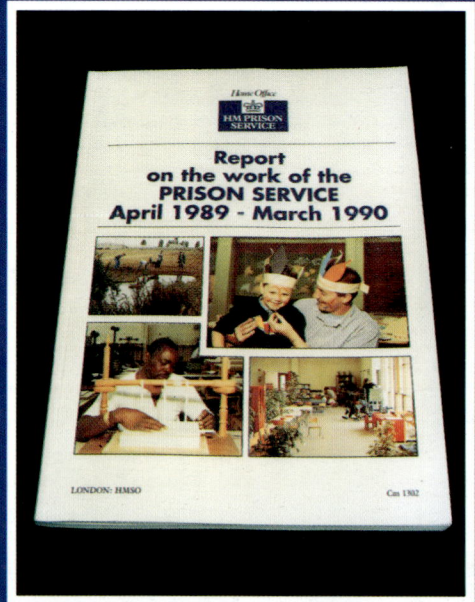

4 Videoconferencing – Prison Service HQ, London

5 The Wolds remand prison – under construction in May 1991

6 Prison Service Annual Report 1989–90

Introduction

3.1   The way the Prison Service is structured can either assist or make more difficult the achievement of its objectives. The structures for conducting relationships between Ministers and the Prison Service, and between headquarters and establishments are important in providing the framework within which good relationships between staff and prisoners can be developed. It is necessary to be clear what the higher level structures are intended to achieve if they are to promote a better prison system.

Purpose

3.2   The organisation and management of prisons should be structured in ways which:

▷   ensure the Prison Service is fully accountable to Ministers for the implementation of the Government's policy for prisons and for the use of the resources entrusted to it;

▷   ensure the Prison Service makes the most effective use of the staff, money and plant at its disposal and so makes the best provision possible for the secure custody and care of prisoners;

▷   enable Governors and their staff to run each establishment effectively in accordance with agreed objectives and within consistent and fair policies;

▷   ensure the public is fully informed of the Prison Service's plans and performance;

▷   allow alternative ways of providing services where these are likely to provide a useful element of competition and good value for money.

Recent Developments

3.3   The Prison Service has introduced far-reaching changes in its structure and management in recent years. These have provided clearer lines of management and accountability, better working practices, and a greatly increased ability to account for its use of resources.

3.4   These changes have included:

▶   The introduction of "Fresh Start" in prison establishments in 1987. "Fresh Start" unified the prison officer and governor grades, changed working practices and abolished prison officer overtime;

▶   reorganisation above establishment level in September 1990. This brought together responsibility for policy development and operational management within three operational Directorates. It provided a direct chain of command through two levels of management from the Governor of each establishment to the Director General;

▶   the restructuring of the published annual report for the Prison Service;

▶   the publication of the inspection and other reports by HM Chief Inspector of Prisons, an independent Inspectorate established by Parliament;

▶   the preparation of a statement on the tasks and functions of the Prison Service. This led to the publication in 1988 of the Statement of Purpose displayed in all Prison Service buildings;

▶   the preparation of an annual planning document for the Prison Service. This sets out the goals and strategy of the Service and the objectives for each year with indicators of success and value for money targets;

▶ the introduction of an annual management contract between the Governor of each establishment and his or her Area Manager. This is intended to establish a clear understanding between the Governor and the line manager of what the establishment is expected to achieve with the resources allocated to it for the coming year. It provides a basis for delegating further responsibilities to Governors;

▶ the establishment of corporate objectives for each establishment. These are intended to define the range of work to be undertaken within each establishment and to provide a clear statement about the level of performance expected for the resources provided.

Future Direction

3.5 The Government wishes to see changes made in the way the relationship between Ministers and the Prison Service is structured, in the relationship between headquarters and prison establishments, and in the way services are provided. The Home Secretary announced in August 1991 that Admiral Sir Raymond Lygo KCB would be conducting a review of the management of the Prison Service. That review will influence the way in which the following proposals relating to the structure of the Prison Service are implemented. Its terms of reference are:

> To review the managerial effectiveness of the Prison Service, both at headquarters and at establishments, with

particular reference to its managerial structures and personnel policies.

Relationship Between Ministers and the Prison Service

3.6 The structure for conducting the relationship between Ministers and the Prison Service must provide the Director General with sufficient authority to manage the Service and to oversee its day to day operations. It must reflect the responsibility of Ministers for the policy and work of the Service. It must meet the expectation of Parliament that Ministers should take a close interest in the way prisoners are treated. In the light of these considerations, the Government's view is that:

▶ **Ministers should continue to remain directly responsible to Parliament** for the policies and objectives of the Service and for the resources made available to it;

▶ **a statement should be published in May each year of the annual objectives of the Service and of the resources which are to be provided for it.** The statement would set out the medium-term goals of the Service and the strategies which it will pursue over time in order to achieve them. It would identify key indicators of success and annual targets. This would form the "compact" between Ministers and the Director General recommended in the Woolf Report. The first such statement would be published next May. The degree to which those objectives have been achieved would be reflected in the following year's annual report;

▶ **the Director General and other**

senior members of the Prison Service should take opportunities to explain in public the Prison Service's performance. Such explanations could cover the Prison Service's performance against its published objectives and relevant day to day operational developments.

Relationship Between Headquarters and Establishments

3.7 Headquarters is and will remain the main channel of communication between Ministers and the Prison Service. Under the Director General, headquarters staff must be able to advise Ministers on policy, and issue the necessary guidance and direction to establishments. At the same time, Governors must be given the discretion to exercise their own judgements and to make a reality of their position as managers of the prison. Their personal authority in the eyes of prisoners will be enhanced if they are seen to be both responsible and accountable for their own establishments.

3.8 There is a balance to be drawn between these considerations. To achieve that balance, the Government intends that:

▶ **headquarters should have an enabling role.** Its work should be directed to enabling Governors to govern their establishments effectively within the policies, strategies and objectives established by Ministers and subject to the resources available. It should provide the advice, assistance and instruction necessary to achieve those ends. It should continue to monitor and seek to improve the performance of establishments and to appraise and develop staff careers to meet operational requirements. Governors should continue to be accountable for the establishment's performance through their headquarters Area Manager. The basis for establishing the Governor's responsibilities and management objectives should continue to be the annual contract between the Governor and the Area Manager. The Prison Service aims to improve the presentation and usefulness of this contract;

▶ **the delegation to Governors of budgetary responsibilities should be extended.** In particular, within the next two years, Governors will have authority to transfer money into their manpower budgets from other running cost provision;

▶ **the delegation to Governors of responsibility for personnel management should be extended.** Local recruitment of non-mobile staff should be the Governor's sole responsibility. Much of the day to day personnel management of prison officers should be conducted by establishments. Starting with the current board, senior officer promotion boards will now be held locally, giving local management a more direct stake in the process;

▶ **the headquarters of the Prison Service should be relocated from London to Derby in 1994.** The decision to relocate from London was announced in January 1990. Relocation will improve headquarters' geographical links with prisons throughout England and Wales and should provide a more cost-effective service;

▶ **there should be a greater interchange of staff between headquarters and prison establishments.** The reorganisation in September 1990 has already resulted in more Governor grades being located in headquarters. The move to Derby should make easier the practical arrangements for interchanging staff;

▶ **communications should be improved between headquarters and establishments.** This will be achieved through regular face-to-face briefing by line managers and by senior management; improved presentation of information for management and staff; a new suggestion scheme open to all staff with better rewards for good ideas and better feedback; and action plans for improving communications in all units and establishments, with relevant objectives incorporated into the Governor's contract with the Area Manager.

Alternative Providers

3.9 The Government considers there is scope for making alternative provision for some aspects of the service at present provided by the Prison Service in England and Wales. The case for this was closely argued during the passage of the Criminal Justice Act 1991. The Government considers that private contractors, if given the opportunity, would be able to provide a high level of service and good value for the taxpayer. The Government has decided that:

▶ **the Wolds remand prison on Humberside will be established under the management of a private sector contractor.** Invitations to tender were sent out in May 1991 and, subject to the receipt of satisfactory tenders, the Government intends to award the contract later in the autumn. The prison would be run by an employee of the contractor, but a Crown Servant would monitor operations on behalf of the Home Secretary. There would be a Board of Visitors and inspections in the normal way. The contract would be specific about the standards of service which were to be met. Once the terms of the contract had been set, however, the private sector contractor would be given the freedom to deliver the required service in the way which made best management sense. Experience with such a contract will enable the Government to determine the scope for further contracting out. It should also help in considering the scope for more extensive delegation to Governors;

▶ **the escorting of prisoners will be contracted out to private sector providers.** The Government considers that the private sector could perform these duties, which are at present undertaken by the police and the Prison Service, to a high standard of efficiency and at a lower cost. Contract performance and the investigation of complaints would be carried out by a monitor appointed by the Home Secretary. Lay observers would be appointed to inspect conditions. The intention is that England and Wales should be divided into ten areas. Detailed examinations are being or will be carried out to determine each area's viability for contracting out. If all areas prove to be viable then, subject to the receipt of satisfactory tenders and an assessment of value for money, over the next few years prison establishments would progressively be relieved of the burden of having to meet escort commitments to the courts. This should help with the planning and predictability of programmes for prisoners and allow the Prison Service to concentrate on its core tasks.

Agency Status

3.10 The Prison Service already has some of the freedoms and flexibilities which are being made available to agencies under the Government's "Next Steps" initiative for the Civil Service. The Prison Service's management practice embraces a number of "Next Steps" ideas, such as clarifying management aims and delegating operational, financial and managerial responsibility. The further delegation proposed in this White Paper, together with the published annual statement of objectives for the Prison Service, take this process a stage further.

3.11 The way the Prison Service is managed has been very significantly changed in recent years. The planned relocation of Prison Service Headquarters to Derby will represent a further major challenge and opportunity for management and staff. This must, for the moment, have priority.

3.12 During the period of relocation the Government intends to develop the structure of the management of the Prison Service progressively in a manner that is consistent with the principles of "Next Steps". It will review the question of when agency status for the Prison Service might be appropriate as the changes set out in this White Paper are introduced. Agency status would have to reflect the Government's view of the extent to which their responsibility for the development of penal policy requires Ministers to take a close interest in what goes on in prisons.

Conclusion

3.13 The proposals in this Chapter should lead to a Prison Service which is structured to provide the best possible service to the public. It will remain directly accountable to Ministers; with published objectives, achieved through clear delegation to Governors in establishments. The purpose of the review announced by the Government will be to strengthen the management of the Prison Service and so ensure that all parts of the Service know what is expected of them and concentrate on that which they can do best.

1 Head of Residential Services (Governor 5) with prisoners – HMP Stocken

2 Personal officer with prisoner – HMP Stocken

3 Management meeting – HMP Frankland

4 Assistant chaplain
leading bible study –
HMP Frankland

5 Prison officer
training – Prison
Service College,
Newbold Revel

Introduction

4.1   The staff of the Prison Service are its most valuable asset. They are the means by which the great majority of services to prisoners are delivered. They are directly responsible for the custody and safe-keeping of prisoners, for their fair treatment and care.

4.2   Prison officers and Governors are at the sharp end of daily dealings with prisoners. But they are part of a wider team. They work together with a wide range of staff in different grades and operational groups, many of whom themselves have close daily contact with prisoners and all of whom make an invaluable contribution to the work of the prison. They need to draw on the assistance of probation officers, on social services and on advice and voluntary agencies working in the community. They require the support, services and instructions of senior management and staff in headquarters, some themselves Governors or former Governors.

4.3   The work of all staff must be directed to meeting the obligations of the Prison Service identified in Chapter 1. Their work must be undertaken sensitively, with maturity and sound judgement, and with respect for the humanity, dignity and individuality of each prisoner. The punishment for sentenced prisoners is the deprivation of their liberty. It is no part of the function of staff to add to that punishment through their attitude or through the way they treat sentenced prisoners. Equally, staff must treat unconvicted prisoners in a way which recognises their legal status.

4.4   These objectives can be achieved only through a well-motivated and well-trained staff dedicated to their work, with a clear sense of purpose and with adequate resources and facilities. They can be achieved only if staff are clear about their duties and deployed in the right way and at the right times – recognising the obligations on a service providing for prisoners 24 hours a day every day of each year.

Present Provision

4.5   The Prison Service has seen a substantial increase in staffing levels, and in the ratio of staff to prisoners in recent years. Since 1987, the number of prison officers in post in establishments has increased by some 4,000, more than 20%. In the same period, the number of other staff in post in establishments has increased by nearly 1,700, also 20% (see Figure 1 overleaf). Since 1979, the increase in prison officers is over 7,400 – 53%. There is now one officer to just over two prisoners: in 1980 there was one officer to three prisoners and in 1950, one officer to six prisoners (changes in these ratios are shown in Figure 2 overleaf).

4.6   The large increases in staffing levels over the last four years have been principally a consequence of the introduction of "Fresh Start", and of the need to staff the additional prison places provided by the Prison Service's extensive building and refurbishment programmes. During this period, the Prison Service has recruited and trained 7,500 new officers. A further 2,500 officers are due to be trained by the end of March 1992. By then, more than twice the number of officers will have been trained in the five years since "Fresh Start" than in the previous five years.

4.7   At the same time, as a consequence of the "Fresh Start" reforms to working practices in prisons introduced in 1987, the number of hours per week which officers work will have reduced from an average of 56 hours in 1987, to an average of 41 hours today, to 39 hours in April 1992. Nevertheless, because of the increase in staffing levels and a fall in the prison population, the number of uniformed staff hours per inmate has increased by 4% since 1987.

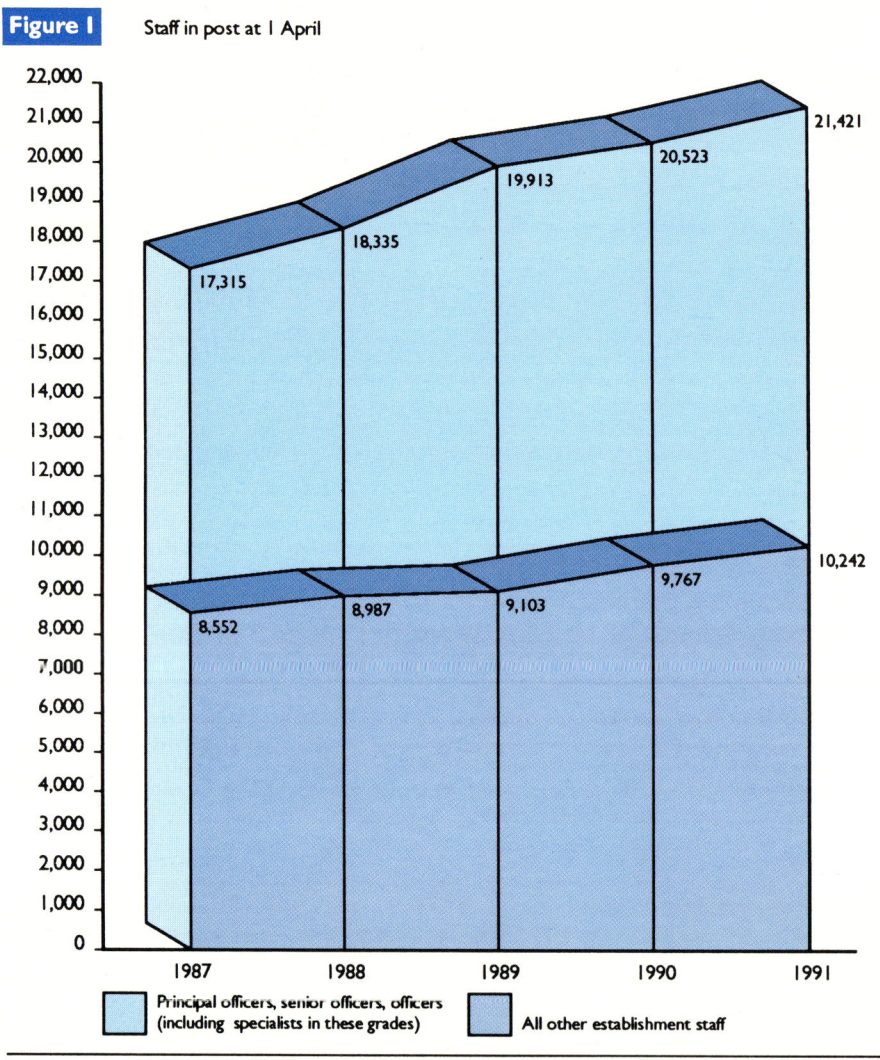

Figure 1 Staff in post at 1 April

Principal officers, senior officers, officers (including specialists in these grades)

All other establishment staff

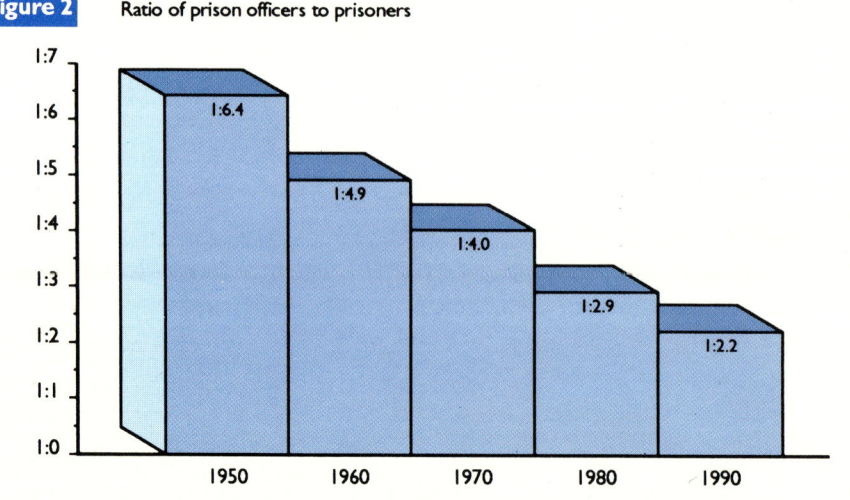

Figure 2 Ratio of prison officers to prisoners

4.8 The Prison Service has through "Fresh Start" improved the terms and conditions for prison officers and governor grades. There is still scope for considerable improvement in personnel policies and in the management of staff. These are matters which will be addressed in the review of the management of the Prison Service referred to in Chapter 3. The implementation of the proposals which follow will take account of this review.

4.9 The Government wishes to enhance the nature and range of the work of prison officers, and to increase their professionalism. Those objectives cannot be achieved in isolation from the work of other staff; it is necessary to improve the jobs of all those in the Prison Service team so that each person can play his or her part flexibly and confidently. The purposes are to improve the way in which staff relate to prisoners and to improve the quality of the service provided. These improvements are essential if the community is to get full value for the money which is invested in the Prison Service.

Staff Recruitment

4.10 The Prison Service selection process concentrates on identifying candidates for appointment as prison officers who show the necessary common sense, adaptability, maturity of judgement and ability to relate sensitively but firmly to others. The requirements for other staff depend on the nature of the tasks they are to undertake and the extent to which they are likely to have contact with prisoners.

4.11 In the coming years, the Government's aim is to ensure that the Prison Service continues to attract suitable staff in the right numbers who, with the necessary training and experience, will be able to make an effective contribution to the running of the Prison Service and hence to the custody and care of prisoners. In particular it will:

▶ **increase the proportion of members of the ethnic minorities in prison officer grades** – by continuing to improve the presentation and direction of its recruiting and monitoring efforts. A governor grade was appointed in May last year as the Prison Service's ethnic minority recruitment officer. He arranges programmes of visits and presentations to community groups and at job centres in areas with high ethnic minority populations. These presentations and visits include valuable contributions from Prison Service staff who are themselves from the ethnic minorities, and who can, therefore, speak from experience. The Prison Service intends over the next few months to improve the monitoring of its performance in retaining staff from the ethnic minorities;

▶ **increase efforts to recruit graduates** – by improving links with universities and colleges;

▶ **review the accelerated promotion scheme** – with a view to attracting candidates with the highest potential from within and outside the Prison Service. This review, which started recently, will take account of the Woolf Report's criticism that successful candidates spend too long in the more junior ranks before becoming Governors and its comments on the desirability of developing the potential of governor grades to enable them to fill the most senior appointments, including that of Director General;

▶ **increase the contribution establishments can make** – by delegating to them the direct recruitment of non-mobile grades and by encouraging them to identify and help to bring forward candidates for appointment as prison officers.

Staff Development

4.12 The Prison Service intends to make full use of all its staff by enabling them to make the best use of their talents. In particular, it will:

▶ **pursue a Better Jobs Initiative.** This has already been announced as a Prisons Board priority for 1991/92 and will continue beyond that period. All Governors and other managers are drawing up programmes in close consultation with their staff which, by the end of this financial year, will have identified practical ways of improving the job satisfaction and the quality of personnel management for all staff in their prison or unit;

▶ **increase the opportunities for providing more fulfilling work for prison officers with prisoners.** There are many examples of such work at present. Officers are involved in throughcare for prisoners and in shared work with probation officers. The NACRO Prison Link Unit provides training for prison officers to run housing and employment advice services in prisons;

▶ **continue to encourage Governors to identify jobs which can be undertaken**

by staff other than prison officers. Many of the previous restrictions have been removed. Governors have the delegated authority, in consultation with their Area Managers, to transfer work to other staff. This frees prison officers for work with prisoners which requires their particular skills and training and provides better jobs for other staff;

▶ **consider the position of staff working in prisons who were not included in the initial "Fresh Start" arrangements.** Their position is not directly comparable with those initially included and it would not be possible, therefore, to offer them a comparable package. They do not have the range of responsibilities of prison officers and Governors. The Prison Service will, however, discuss with staff in these other grades and their representative bodies whether they consider there is scope for financing improvements in pay or allowances through efficiency savings, following the principles of "Fresh Start". The Prison Service will consider also whether there are other measures which, within available resources, will improve the jobs and conditions of these staff;

▶ **produce a new handbook for all staff setting out standards for the treatment and care of prisoners.** The handbook will provide staff with guidance about the practical implementation of those standards, especially at sensitive points during a person's time in prison – for example on reception, in segregation, when ill and when the prisoner might present a suicide risk. It will encourage the sensitive treatment of the prisoner's family and help managers to assess and improve the quality of care provided by staff;

▶ **issue shortly a new Guide for Line Managers on Service Induction with a clearer and more readable Guide for New Staff**;

▶ **provide staff in prisons with a statement of the facilities for and the standards expected of them.** This statement would be piloted in selected establishments from the beginning of the next financial year. It would be a form of the staff "compact" recommended in the Woolf Report. It would be provided by the Governor to his or her staff, after consultation with them. The aim would be to review its operation after 12 months and, subject to that review, to extend statements to staff in all establishments;

▶ **continue to improve the performance of all staff in treating prisoners fairly and without discrimination on grounds of race or religion** – in accordance with the Prison Service's published statement on race relations policy displayed in all establishments. The Prison Service intends to build on the new Race Relations Manual and the local training pack which were issued in April 1991. A revised pocket book on race relations was issued to all staff in July this year. Governors will identify what improvements should be made at their establishments and include those in their annual contracts with their Area Managers. The Prison Service will seek to improve its monitoring and reporting of racial incidents;

▶ **introduce a Prison Officer Development Scheme.** This will provide earlier opportunities for promotion and therefore more attractive career prospects for staff with particular potential for advancement;

▶ **increase the posting of female staff to male establishments and vice versa.** This has been shown to assist in the effective management of both male and female establishments and to enhance the jobs of the staff involved. The Prison Service will work to develop such postings in the interests of the staff, prisoners and the performance of the Service;

▶ **broaden the experience of Prison Service staff** – by exploring the scope for seconding Prison Service and other Home Office staff to other criminal justice agencies and vice versa; and by developing exchanges with other public services and commercial organisations.

Staff Training

4.13 A well-trained staff is essential if the Prison Service is to provide a good and cost-effective service. Training needs to be carefully planned and assessed. When the main pressures for training newly recruited staff ease towards the end of this year, there will be scope to concentrate more on in-service training. To these ends, the Prison Service will:

▶ **provide accreditation for the initial training courses for prison officers** and will consider whether it would be helpful to provide opportunities for officers to work towards achieving national vocational qualifications for key aspects of their jobs;

▶ **improve the training which locally recruited staff receive when they join an establishment.** Some establishments already provide excellent induction training. The aim will be to spread good practice by providing guidance to establishments on the elements which should be included in induction programmes;

▶ **complete its review of in-service training provision** – to identify what further provision might be required, how take-up can be improved, and the consequent resource and staffing implications. This review began in March 1989 and will be completed by March 1992. The work has already led to the development of new modules for management training which are designed to count towards external qualifications, and to a five day foundation course with 20 days follow-up training for newly promoted Governor 5s. The present course for senior governors is being replaced by a more broadly based programme of senior management studies and from October 1991 there will be a course specifically for governors taking charge of establishments for the first time. By March 1992, the aim is to have prepared a full training strategy for the Service;

▶ **explore the scope for increasing shared training with other criminal justice agencies**, in particular with members of the probation service.

Staffing Levels

4.14 The Government wishes to see introduced a more rigorous and objective method of assessing staffing levels. It should be possible to establish a link between the investment in staff resources and the results achieved. It is for the Government to decide what resources can be made available to the Prison Service in the light of its consideration of priorities for public expenditure. But these decisions, and decisions about the way the Prison Service's resources are allocated, can be more firmly based if there is a more systematic analysis of the work of establishments and what could be achieved for the particular level of resources which may be provided.

4.15 To meet these objectives, the Prison Service has introduced a system of work identification and resource planning under the corporate objectives process. This has allowed each prison establishment progressively to address these complex and inter-related issues. The Government hopes that discussions with the Prison Officers' Association will result in the Association lifting its advice to its local branches not to co-operate with this proccess. Meanwhile, the process is being carried forward and is due to be completed this autumn. The information provided by that exercise should enable the Service to assess:

▶ the staffing levels required in each establishment during the week and at weekends for particular levels of regime activity;

▶ the likely implications for staffing levels and for staff deployment in providing more active regimes for prisoners;

▶ the scope for extending civilianisation of work at present undertaken by prison officers and governor grades;

▶ the scope for extending part-time working so that, for example, former prison officers now bringing up a family or who have left to pursue other interests might be attracted to work part-time for the Prison Service.

4.16 The result of this should be a clearer understanding of the nature of the work to be performed in each prison, who is available to perform it and the times when and the ways in which it can be undertaken most effectively. It will ensure that available resources are used to best effect. The case for any additional staff must be founded on that assurance and on the Prison Service's ability to show a closer relationship between the resources provided and what is actually achieved.

Uniforms

4.17 The Government recognises that what staff wear reflects what the Prison Service is there to do and the way it is expected to do it. There is no reason to believe that the wearing of a suitable and non-threatening uniform affects the way prisoners relate to staff – the personality is more important than the clothing. The uniform must however be suitable to the role which officers are there to perform.

4.18 The prison officer's job requires a well-judged mix of caring for prisoners and of ensuring their security and control. Governors provide both operational leadership and management for prison officers and for all other staff working in the prison. The Governor is the head of a team and must ensure that the team works together. The clothes worn by Governors, prison officers and other staff need to be considered in the context of these different functions and tasks.

4.19 These are matters which require consideration in consultation with staff and their representatives. That consultation needs to take account of the practical and resource considerations. It must take account also of the nature of the Prison Service which is needed in the years ahead. The Prison Service will, therefore, shortly start on a review of the purposes of wearing uniforms and how best these can be met. The Service will consider the most appropriate wear for staff in the light of that review, including the case for moving to a less militaristic style of uniform and the scope for greater discretion about wearing uniform, as proposed in the Woolf Report.

4.20 There are, however, some matters on which action can be taken in advance of the review. The Government intends that all staff on duty in prisons, whether in uniform or not, should wear badges showing their name and rank or job title. It will consult staff and their representatives about the implementation of this policy. The Prison Service has also:

▶ confirmed to establishments the rules against cutting the peaks of caps and instructed Governors to provide for their early replacement where they have been so defaced;

▶ instructed that officers working within establishments should not wear uniform caps or hats except where required for protection from the weather;

► confirmed that prison issue pullovers are a fully acceptable alternative to tunics for day to day wear in prisons;

► made provision for those working in prisons during a disturbance to wear overalls to protect their clothing.

Industrial Relations

4.21 The Prison Service seeks to promote and foster good industrial relations with its staff. The following principles were set out for all staff in a policy statement issued in September 1989:

▷ management has a duty to use resources effectively and efficiently while all members of staff look for satisfaction in their work, a safe and secure working environment and reasonable material rewards. Both have a common interest in the stability as well as the efficiency of the Service since, without it, neither can fully achieve their aims;

▷ good industrial relations are the joint responsibility of management, trade unions and individual members of staff. Management recognises and accepts its responsibilities to promote good relations;

▷ conflicts of interest are bound to arise from time to time but the objective should be for conflict to be resolved in a timely, responsible and constructive way and at the lowest possible level in the organisation;

▷ in pursuing good industrial relations there will be occasions when management cannot concede to trade union demands. Management does not seek confrontation

but on occasion it will need to stand firm.

4.22 The Prison Service will continue to conduct industrial relations policy in accordance with these principles. It will continue to seek with the trade unions effective arrangements for consultation and communication, and for the settling of grievances and disputes. Where industrial action is taken, the Prison Service will seek to resolve the dispute in the interests of all those involved. The Government supports the proposal in the Woolf Report that the nationally agreed disputes procedure should include a commitment to refrain from industrial action until the procedure has been exhausted. The Prison Service will consult the Prison Officers' Association to seek the Association's agreement to the incorporation of this in the procedure.

4.23 The Government is concerned about the frequency and seriousness of industrial action in the Prison Service. It agrees with the Woolf Report's view that it is not for the Prison Officers' Association to determine the proper maximum accommodation in a prison, or to seek to enforce such a decision through refusing to admit prisoners and so subject them to police cells. Such action reflects on the professionalism and standing of the Service; it causes considerable distress to prisoners and their families, and to other staff in the Prison Service; it puts increased burdens and costs on others in the criminal justice system, including the police; and it affects the ability of the criminal justice system to act effectively in the maintenance of law and order in this country.

4.24 The Government considers that the proposals set out in this White Paper have the potential substantially to transform the nature of the prison system in the years ahead. In making these proposals, the Government has given considerable weight to improving the conditions, status and work of staff in the Prison Service. The pace of change will, however, depend on a matching contribution and commitment from Prison Service staff and from the unions who represent them. Accordingly, the Prison Service will establish bi-lateral and joint discussions with all the Prison Service unions to see if a consensus can be established on how industrial relations can be improved.

Conclusion

4.25 This Chapter has set out the improvements the Government wishes to see in the way Prison Service staff are recruited, developed, trained and deployed in the years ahead. The Government believes its aims should be shared by the Prison Service unions since the unions share the Government's commitment to a more professional Prison Service providing high standards of care to prisoners in a secure environment. But their achievement will depend on there being a sea change in industrial relations in the Prison Service. Without such a change, there can be no assurance that the resources devoted to the Prison Service will be used effectively and efficiently in a way which fulfils the obligations of the Prison Service. The Government is ready to play its part in bringing about that change.

1

2

3

1 and 2 Headquarters Tactical Management
and Planning Unit – Birmingham

3 Remand Centre – HMRC Low Newton

4

5

4 Female
establishment –
HMP Holloway

5 Local prison –
HMP Durham

6 New generation
prison under
construction –
Milton Keynes

6

Introduction

5.1 The management of the prison population – the way in which the prisoners are assigned to establishments – is one of the most complex tasks in the Prison Service. It raises daily logistical problems. It requires careful long-term planning. Decisions made about the allocation of the prison population affect directly individual prisoners, their families, the Prison Service's own staff, and the communities in which the prisons are situated.

5.2 A doctrinaire approach to these questions will not do. The range of individual circumstances is too great. There are disadvantages as well as advantages to most plans. The unpredictability of many of the factors which influence the nature of the prison population from day to day requires a flexible response. Long-term plans also must recognise that flexibility is necessary to meet changing circumstances.

5.3 Flexibility must however operate within a set of clear principles and priorities and in accordance with a clearly established direction. The Prison Service must know where it is going in the way it manages its prison population. It must use its wisdom and ingenuity to maintain that course.

Aims

5.4 The Prison Service has the following aims in deciding on the allocation of prisoners. They are:

▷ to hold prisoners in establishments which provide the degree of security which they require;

▷ to manage the population to make best use of the available accommodation;

▷ to avoid recourse to police cells because suitable accommodation cannot be found in prison establishments;

▷ to reduce overcrowding – and in particular to avoid having to hold three prisoners in cells designed for one;

▷ to hold prisoners in establishments which are near to their homes, or for unconvicted and unsentenced prisoners, near to the courts dealing with their cases;

▷ to hold those prisoners who have particular identified needs in establishments which can provide for them;

▷ to hold prisoners in establishments suitable to their gender, age and legal status.

5.5 These aims are not easily reconciled and in many cases may be irreconcilable. Those requiring the highest levels of security for long periods are unlikely to have as good a chance of being held near to their homes and families as prisoners with less demanding requirements. Prisoners wanting to benefit from particular regimes – for example the education programme at Sudbury/Foston prison – may have to choose between that or staying nearer to their homes. Open prisons are not easily or sensibly sited in the centre of urban communities – prisoners benefiting from their more relaxed and open regimes may have to live away from their home areas. Under present circumstances, the more groups have to be held entirely separately – remands from sentenced, young offenders from adults, women from men, those serving long sentences from those serving much shorter ones – the greater is the likelihood that overcrowding in one group cannot be relieved by transferring the prisoners elsewhere.

5.6   The prison estate needs to be managed flexibly, but it is inherently inflexible. It has been built up over the last 200 years – it cannot be rebuilt in the space of a few years. Many establishments are located in parts of the country which are remote from the main centres of population – they cannot be relocated overnight. There are options for increasing the security level in an establishment, or for changing its use from holding one type of prisoner to holding another. But that takes time and money. There may also be planning or other considerations arising from undertakings given to the local community that may narrow those options.

5.7   The estate contains a number of large prisons in city centres – ideally situated, but not ideally built. Many prisoners prefer to stay in such prisons, near to their homes and their legal advisers, despite the cramped conditions. Substantially reducing the scale of these prisons, even if the cost could be justified, would increase the number of prisoners who would have to be moved away from their home areas.

5.8   Any plans for changing the use of prisons and the management of the prison population must take account of these factors.

Current Position

5.9   There have been major changes in the nature of the prison population over the last 30 years. The prison estate has been adapted to meet these changes and has been very considerably improved and extended, particularly in the last ten years. The main developments are shown in the following tables and graphs:

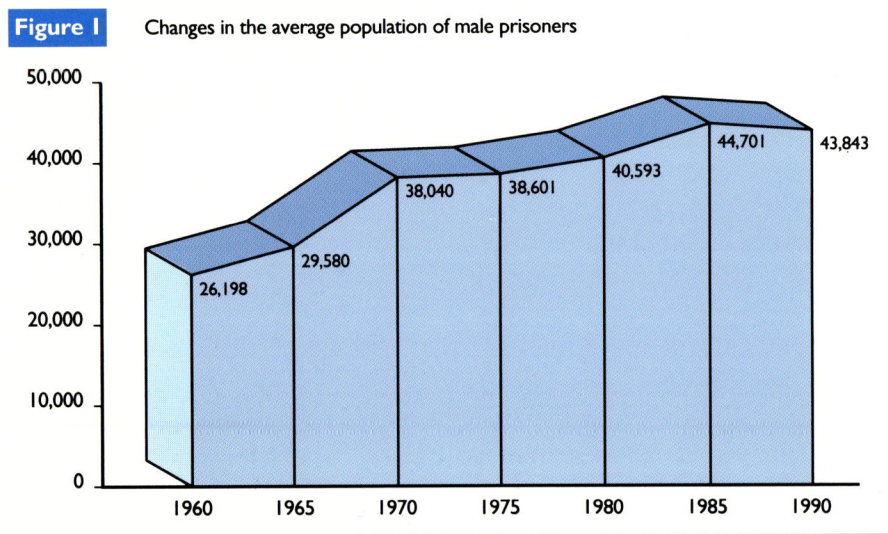

Figure 1   Changes in the average population of male prisoners

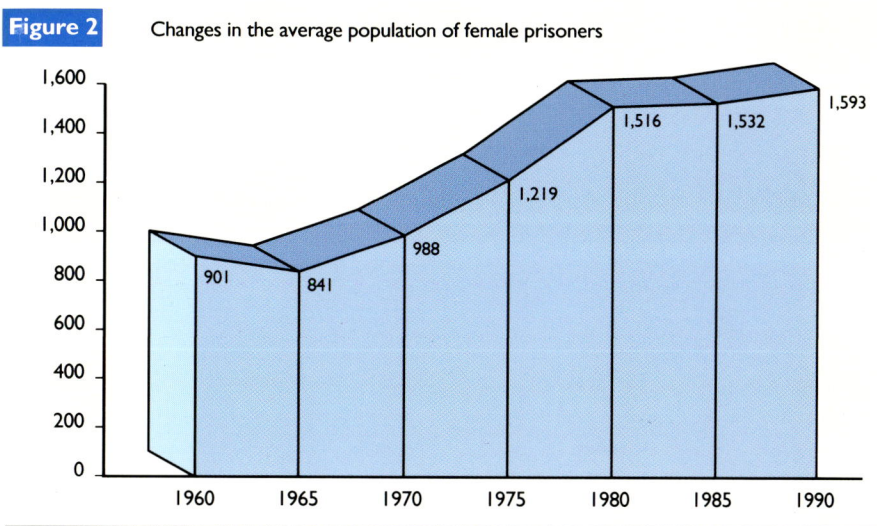

Figure 2   Changes in the average population of female prisoners

Figure 3   Changes in the types of male prisoner

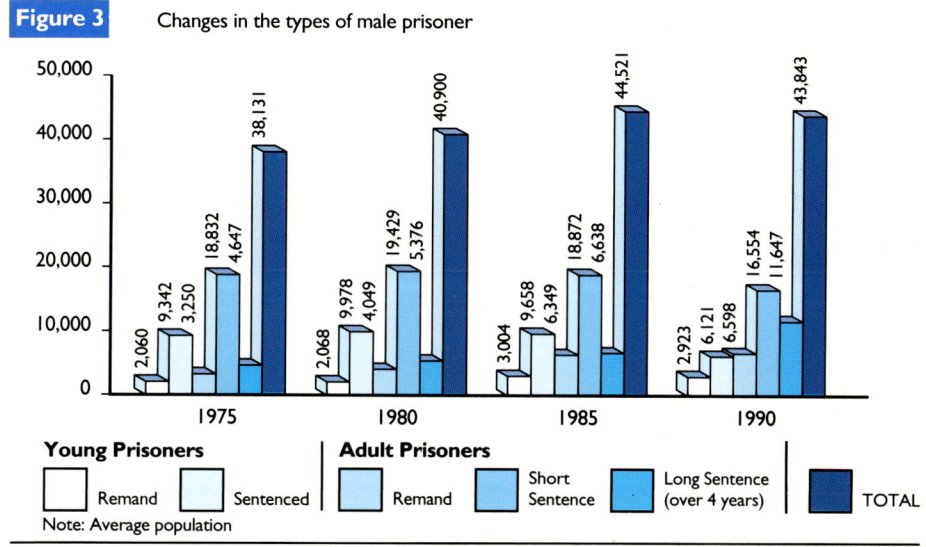

Young Prisoners   **Adult Prisoners**

☐ Remand   ☐ Sentenced   ☐ Remand   ☐ Short Sentence   ☐ Long Sentence (over 4 years)   ■ TOTAL

Note: Average population

Figure 4   Changes in the types of female prisoner

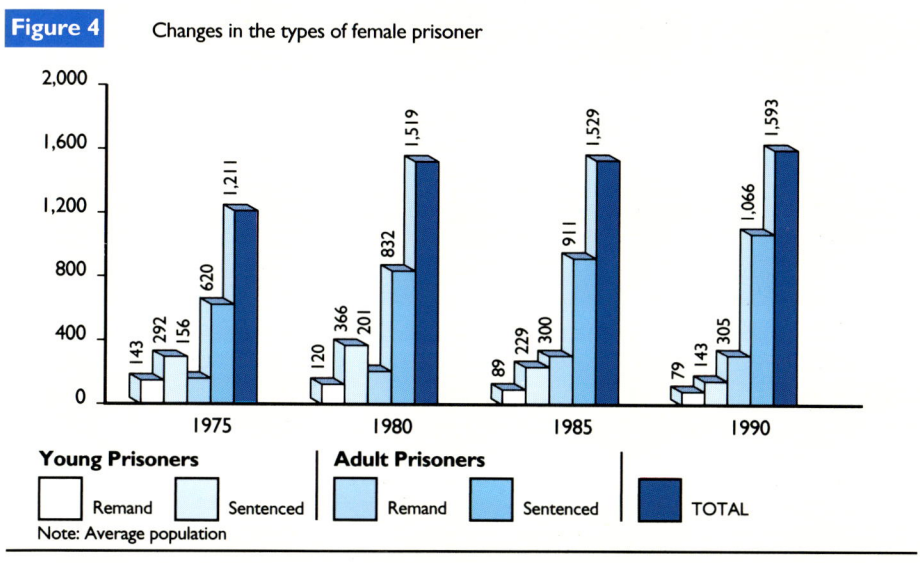

Young Prisoners   **Adult Prisoners**

☐ Remand   ☐ Sentenced   ☐ Remand   ☐ Sentenced   ■ TOTAL

Note: Average population

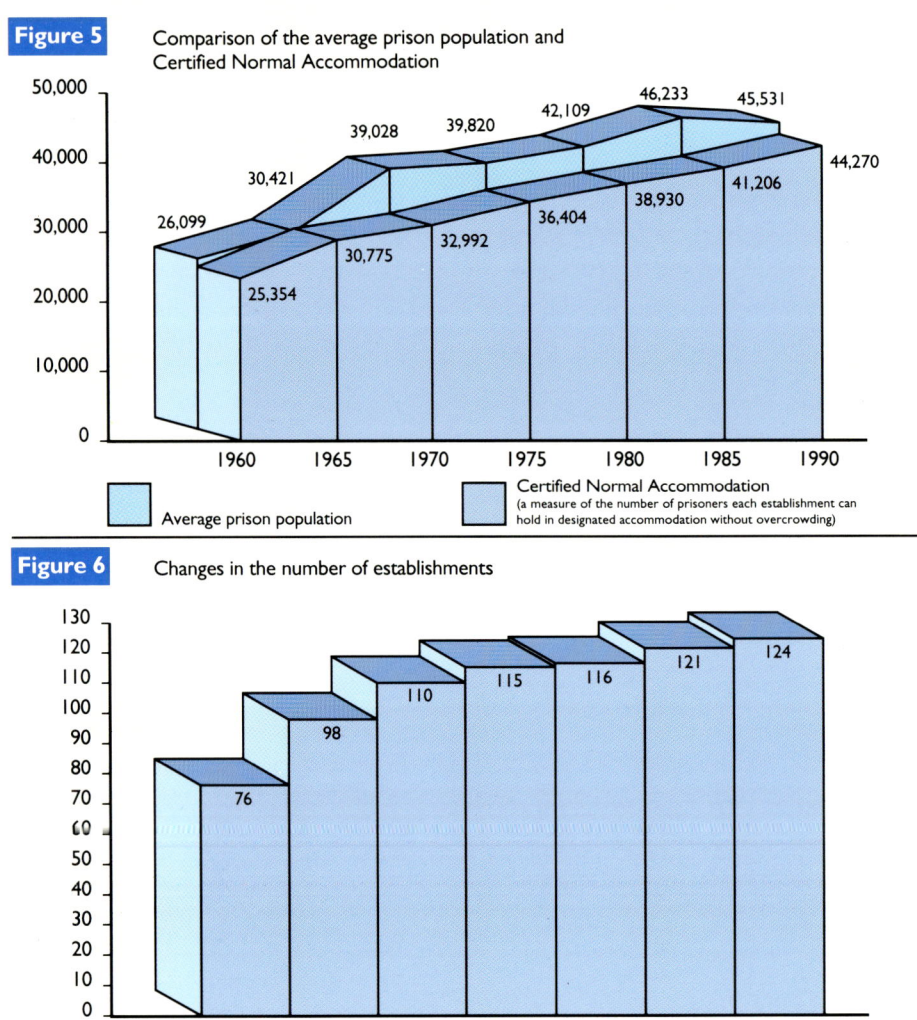

Figure 5   Comparison of the average prison population and Certified Normal Accommodation

Average prison population

Certified Normal Accommodation (a measure of the number of prisoners each establishment can hold in designated accommodation without overcrowding)

Figure 6   Changes in the number of establishments

5.10 There have been changes too in the way allocation decisions are made, and the way long-term planning is organised. Since September 1990, the arrangements for allocating prisoners, and the long-term planning of the prison estate have been brought together in a headquarters tactical management and planning unit under the Director of Custody. This has established a closer link between planning and daily operations; and it enables the system to be planned nationally without artificial regional or area boundaries.

5.11 There are also other changes and improvements in prospect. Since 1979, the Government has invested £1,036m in a major building and refurbishment programme including, so far, bringing ten new prisons into use providing over 4,500 places. Between now and 1994 a further 11 prisons will be commissioned, providing accommodation for nearly 6,300 prisoners. Ten of these new prisons are intended to be used as local prisons or remand centres. Building work in existing establishments has since 1979 provided nearly

4,000 additional places and by 1995 will provide a further 2,000 places.

5.12 At the same time, the Prison Service keeps under regular review its use of existing prisons in the light of current and anticipated requirements. As a result, the role of some establishments is changed to meet changing requirements and the opportunity is taken to close others, in particular where the quality of accommodation provided is unsuitable. Following the Woolf Report, reviews are based on geographical clusters of establishments and take account of the need to locate prisoners close to their homes as well as the need to take unsuitable accommodation out of the estate.

Future Direction

5.13 The future direction for the management of the prison population requires clear objectives and priorities. The Government considers these objectives should be as follows and in the following order of priority:

▶   every effort should be made to avoid prisoners who should be accommodated in prisons being held in police cells, even if that requires an element of overcrowding in prisons;

▶   the prison population and the existing estate should be managed in a way which avoids having to hold prisoners in overcrowded conditions – provided that the achievement of this objective does not require individual prisoners to be relocated frequently from one establishment to another for that reason alone;

▶   where this can be achieved within the existing estate, prisoners should be located in prisons suitable to their status and security category as near to their homes as possible, unless they request otherwise, or their behaviour or the management of their sentences requires it. Location near to home is likely to lead to greater stability in prisons and will enable programmes to be linked more closely to the opportunities available to the prisoner after release. Provisional information from the National Prison Survey (1) tends to confirm that the vast majority of prisoners attach considerable importance to being in a prison near family and friends.

5.14 For young offenders, unconvicted prisoners and women prisoners, these priorities will be influenced by the following considerations:

▶   it is preferable that young offenders and unconvicted prisoners on remand should be located in less crowded conditions with prisoners of a different status than that they should be held separately in overcrowded conditions. Neither group should be required, however, to share cells, rooms or dormitories with other types of prisoners;

▶   it is preferable that women prisoners should be located as near to their homes as possible: where the location of female establishments is particularly poor, it may be necessary, after full consultation both within and outside the Prison Service, to consider the possibility of accommodating women prisoners in establishments shared with male prisoners, provided the accommodation is separate, fully secure and of an adequate size, and that the women will have satisfactory facilities and regime activities.

5.15 In the longer term, these priorities should be influenced by the following developments:

▶ as the building and refurbishment programme proceeds, and where the location of existing establishments makes this possible, there should be groups or clusters of prisons able to hold prisoners of most types and security categories. The aim should be for prisoners from the locality served by the cluster of prisons to spend most of their time in custody within that locality. Wherever possible, such a cluster of prisons should provide separate establishments for women, remand prisoners, young male offenders and adult men;

▶ clusters should be centred around local prisons. More will need to be identified. Local prisons will be adapted over the coming years to fill their new role as the hub of the community system, or, in some cases, as multi-functional prisons holding a wide range of prisoners for most or all of their time in custody;

▶ refurbishment programmes should, over the coming years, provide for the division of large wings in establishments into smaller units. The provision of these units will help the creation of multi-functional community prisons by enabling them to hold different groups of prisoners in separate living units. Smaller units should also assist in developing constructive relationships between staff and prisoners and should provide the opportunity to offer more flexible regimes better suited

to the prisoners they hold. It should be possible to create conditions equivalent to security Category C establishments in some units. Ideally the units should each hold between 50 and 70 prisoners, but design and resource considerations are likely to lead to larger sized units in particular cases. Units of between 50 to 70 prisoners have, however, been the basis for most new accommodation built for the Prison Service since the 1950s and all prisons now under construction have units of this size;

▶ the concept of multi-functional community prisons would be helped if large prisons were organised in managerially discrete groups of living units. Accordingly, refurbishment programmes in large prisons will, over the coming years, consider providing accommodation areas holding, ideally, some 400 prisoners. In most cases, prisons arranged in this way would still need to share common facilities, such as workshops, the gymnasium, visiting facilities and the health care centre. The possibility of prisons at present under construction being managed in groups of this size will also be considered. In many cases, however, larger numbers are likely to be necessary because of design and resource considerations.

5.16 The full exposition of this policy will necessarily take many years to complete. It will, however, guide the Prison Service in the allocation decisions which it makes; it will influence the regular reviews of the estate which it undertakes; and it will guide its future refurbishment and rebuilding programmes. In the immediate future, as steps on the way towards achieving this policy, the Government will:

▶ **identify a number of existing and new local prisons which might be replanned as multi-functional community prisons;**

▶ **consider whether there are existing prisons which could be more directly linked to a local prison** so that a prisoner's sentence plan could provide for the prisoner to progress mainly through that cluster of establishments.

The Management of Remand Prisoners

5.17 The Government recognises the separate legal status of unconvicted prisoners. It is reflected in the Prison Rules and in the European Prison Rules. The Prison Service's provision should reflect the legal position of unconvicted prisoners as people who are presumed innocent unless and until found guilty.

5.18 It is not in principle desirable that those who have been held for the purpose of bringing their case to court should be required to share accommodation and spend their time with prisoners who have been convicted or sentenced to prison as a punishment. Experience has shown that where an establishment has had to provide for both convicted and unconvicted prisoners, more attention has been given to the requirements of convicted and sentenced prisoners whose period in prison is more predictable and who may be more ready and able to use the opportunities provided.

5.19 The Government's policy therefore is to establish separate centres for remand prisoners. The Government proposes to work towards this by building such centres on separate sites, and on sites shared with other establishments, as resources allow. This will necessarily be a long-term programme. In the meantime, the Prison Service will aim to locate unconvicted prisoners in living units separate from convicted prisoners, subject to the priorities which have been identified in the previous section.

5.20 Remand prisoners are at present not normally given a security classification. Other than those given a provisional categorisation at the highest level of security – Category A – remand prisoners are unclassified, but are presumed to require Category B conditions. There is no evidence or reason to believe that prisoners remanded in custody by the courts can, as a group, be held securely in Category C conditions. Nor are there at present or in the foreseeable future likely to be sufficient Category C establishments conveniently located for such prisoners.

5.21 It would, however, be consistent with the principle that prisoners should be held in no greater or lesser degree of security than they require, and enable greater flexibility in the use of the prison estate, if all remand prisoners were given a security categorisation in the same way as sentenced prisoners. This would allow more informed judgements to be made about the degree of risk presented by each prisoner.

5.22 The Home Secretary announced on 5 August 1991 that the Prison Service would review by the end of October the current policy for the classification and treatment of remand prisoners at present given a provisional Category A classification. In addition, the Prison Service aims, in consultation with the police, to introduce a system which will enable all male and female remand prisoners to be given a security categorisation. Such a system may influence the way lower category prisoners are accommodated in Category B establishments, and the regime opportunities available to them. It would also enable the Prison Service to consider in future reviews of its estate whether there are some Category C prisons, or parts of Category C prisons, which could hold remand prisoners.

The Management of Vulnerable and Sex Offenders

5.23   The Prison Service has a general duty of care and, if necessary, protection for all the prisoners in its custody. The aim should be to exercise such care at all times and to ensure that vulnerable prisoners, including those who have been convicted of certain sexual offences, are given the same quality of opportunity as any other prisoner. When a prisoner is victimised, the aim should be to restrict the victimiser and not the victim.

5.24   The Government looks to the development of the policies set out in this White Paper to provide a climate in prisons where these objectives become more easily achievable. In particular, there is some evidence that prisoners who receive a fuller and more positive regime are less likely to take the risk of losing it by victimising other prisoners.

5.25   For the time being, however, it will remain necessary to make particular provision for some male sex offenders. It is not at present reasonable to leave these prisoners without special protection. They also should have the opportunity to face up to their crimes. The Prison Service therefore intends to allocate sex offenders to one of up to 20 prisons. The Prison Service's intentions in preparing programmes for such offenders are described in Chapter 7. As a consequence, this allocation requirement will take priority over the general objectives described above for the management and allocation of the prison population.

5.26   There will continue to be circumstances in which a vulnerable prisoner has to be segregated from other prisoners in his or her own interests. The purpose of such segregation should be to provide time for prison management to assess the situation and decide on the best way of handling it. No prisoner should be segregated for longer than is absolutely necessary. It should be possible for prison management to demonstrate throughout that period that active steps are being taken to remove the prisoner from segregation and locate him or her more appropriately. It is a responsibility of the Board of Visitors to monitor that situation.

5.27   The Government accepts the proposal in the Woolf Report that the existing Rule 43 (and Young Offender Institution Rule 46) should be amended to apply only to prisoners removed from association in the interests of the good order or discipline of the establishment and not also to prisoners removed from association in their own interests. The Government will amend the present rules and introduce separate rules to make clear the Governor's responsibilities and powers in respect of vulnerable prisoners.

The Management of Disruptive Prisoners

5.28   The Prison Service must be able to hold securely highly disruptive prisoners. Staff must have the skills necessary to deal with disruptive behaviour. There can be no excuse or justification for the use of unnecessary force, intimidation or other unprofessional behaviour against such prisoners. The aim should be to avoid over-reacting; and to avoid taking action which unnecessarily labels the prisoner as permanently disruptive and so gets him or her into a cycle of misbehaviour and punishment from which it is not easy to escape.

5.29 Wherever possible, and as a normal practice, each establishment should deal with those who behave in an unco-operative or disruptive fashion from within its own resources and by use of its own accommodation. The judicious and limited use of segregation will remain an important resource to establishments. But this must be seen and used as a last resort. The way prisoners are treated on segregation requires close supervision by line management and regular and independent monitoring by members of Boards of Visitors.

5.30 There are likely to continue to be occasions where, despite the best efforts of the establishment, and despite the improved conditions and programmes presaged in this White Paper, a prisoner has to be relocated outside the establishment, for at least a period. The particular arrangements for transfers set out in Circular Instruction 37/1990, and generally endorsed in the Woolf Report, will, therefore, continue. As that circular makes clear, such transfers should be used sparingly. The local prison to which a prisoner is transferred should seek to assess the prisoner's behaviour and the reasons for it and seek to resolve, as far as possible, the difficulties which the prisoner perceives.

5.31 It should be possible for persistently disruptive prisoners serving long sentences to be considered for allocation to one of the special units established following the Prison Service's Control Review Committee Report of 1984 (2). It should not be the practice for disruptive prisoners to be transferred from one prison to another at frequent intervals in order to control their behaviour or reduce its effects on any particular establishment. Such action is likely only to exacerbate disruptive behaviour and increase feelings of victimisation.

5.32 The Government accepts that segregation for reasons of good order or discipline under Rule 43 (or Rule 46 of the Young Offender Institution Rules) is a substantial decision which may have a marked, and sometimes traumatic, effect on the prisoner. So too is a transfer to another establishment for the same reasons (whether or not under the specific arrangements of Circular Instruction 37/1990). The arrangements require careful monitoring by management and Boards of Visitors. The Government accepts that the prisoner should wherever possible be given the reasons for these decisions in writing.

5.33 It will, therefore, continue to be necessary to allocate a small number of disruptive prisoners at short notice to a local prison for a limited period, or, after longer consideration, to a special unit. Those requirements will, for them, take priority over the general objectives described above for the management and allocation of the prison population as a whole.

Conclusion

5.34 This Chapter sets out a planned programme of developments and change for the management of the prison population. It gives high priority to reducing overcrowding. It recognises the advantages of holding prisoners in small living units in multi-functional community prisons or in groups of prisons near to their homes and families. It recognises that some prisoners need special allocation which takes precedence over these objectives. It is a long-term programme which will in time transform the management of our prisons – and which is already influencing day to day allocation decisions.

Notes

(1) The National Prison Survey was conducted by the Office of Population Censuses and Surveys between January and March 1991. It was commissioned on behalf of the Prison Service by the Home Office Research and Planning Unit. The analysis of its results will be completed later this year.

(2) "Managing the Long-Term Prison System", The Report of the Control Review Committee, HMSO, July 1984.

Chapter 6

1

1 Prisoners and officer – HMP Belmarsh

2 Installing integral sanitation – HMP Birmingham

3 Stainless steel sanitation unit in place – HMP Birmingham

2

3

4

4 Food
preparation – HMP
Stocken

5 The prison
hospital – HMP
Winchester

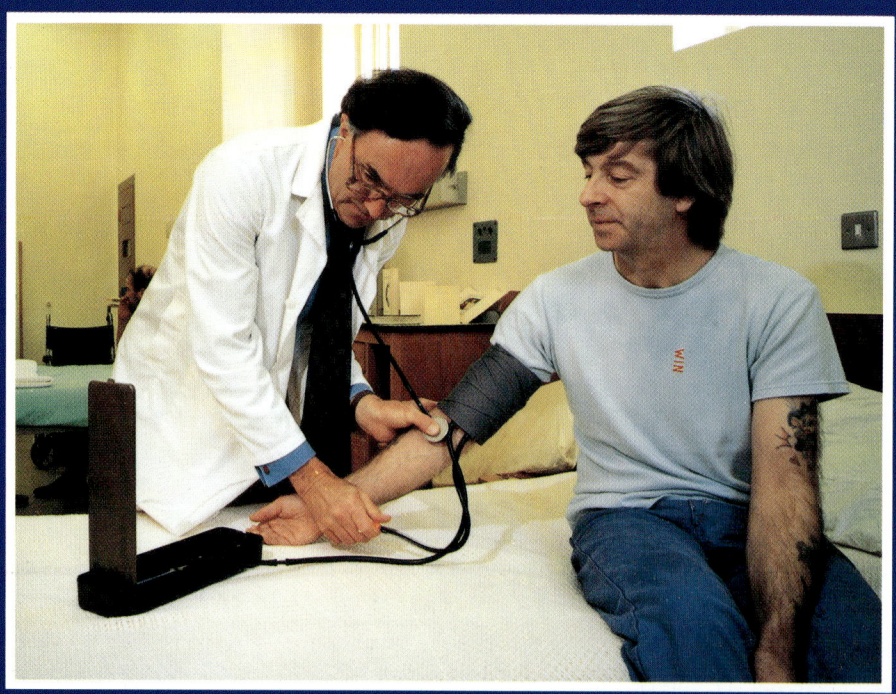

5

Introduction

6.1 Prisons should aim to provide decent but not lavish conditions. Conditions should be of a standard which fulfils the Prison Service's duty to provide humanely for prisoners and to preserve human dignity. They should provide an environment in which both prisoners and staff are motivated to work together positively to make the best use of a prisoner's time in prison. They should sustain prisoners: they should not degrade them.

6.2 Conditions in prisons had, for many years, failed to meet these objectives. Buildings were predominately Victorian. The conditions were Dickensian. The number of places available had not kept pace with the number of prisoners in custody.

6.3 Since 1979, the Government's building and refurbishment programmes referred to in Chapter 5 have provided additional accommodation and improved conditions for prisoners, their visitors and for staff.

6.4 The result on the overall quality of prisons has been marked. In 1960, 67% of prison places were provided in prisons built during or before the Victorian period. In 1991, it is 39%. Older prisons however will continue to have a valuable role to play in providing accommodation for prisoners. Many were soundly constructed and are very well located near the communities they serve. The refurbishment programme has been aimed at bringing them, together with some more modern constructions, up to current standards.

6.5 It would be wrong to characterise all prisons as holding too many prisoners in conditions which fail to meet current standards, or to suggest that there have been no improvements in recent years. The Prison Service has estimated that in 1960 half of all prisoners had to be held in overcrowded conditions. By 1991, it was less than one third. In 1960, only 33% of places had full access to sanitation. It was to remain like that until 1980. By the end of this financial year, over 70% will have full access to sanitation.

6.6 These figures show the progress which has been made. They show also that there is much still to be achieved. The need is particularly great in local prisons and remand centres.

Access to Sanitation

6.7 The Government shares the view of the Woolf Report, and of successive Chief Inspectors of Prisons, that priority should be given to providing sanitation for all prisoners. Provisional information from the National Prison Survey (1) suggests that prisoners give a higher priority to having a lavatory in their cells than to reducing overcrowding. The Woolf Report recommended that there should be full access to sanitation by February 1996 at the latest. The Home Secretary announced on 25 February 1991, that a further £18m would be provided to the Prison Service so that every prisoner would have full access to sanitation by the end of 1994. He announced that the cost of this programme over the next four years was an extra £36m.

6.8 From the end of December 1994, therefore, all prisoners in Prison Service establishments will have access to sanitation at all times, either in their own cells or, at night, by the use of electronic locks which allow them to go from their cells to the lavatory. The scale of this work will inevitably involve a temporary loss of places and therefore short-term pressures, but the work will be carried out as speedily as possible. The temporary pressures on prison places will be more than justified by the assurance that no prisoner will have to endure the inhumane and degrading practice of slopping out after the end of 1994.

Overcrowding

6.9 The Prison Service does not have the same control over the number of prisoners coming into the system as it does over the provision of sanitation for them. Prisons must cater for all those sent to them. The size of the prison population is determined by the daily decisions of the courts, interpreting the legislation passed by Parliament.

6.10 The problem of overcrowding, particularly in local prisons, has been a drain on the Prison Service over many years. It has made it very difficult to provide acceptable conditions. It engenders tension amongst staff as well as prisoners and their families. It puts pressure not just on cell accommodation, but also on many of the other facilities in the prison. A decent service depends on the end of overcrowding.

6.11 The Government accepts therefore that the objective should be that no prisoner should have to be accommodated in overcrowded conditions. The achievement of this objective needs careful planning, taking account of the following factors:

▶ **cell sharing.** Wherever possible, prisoners should not be required to share cells. But some cell sharing will still be appropriate, to meet prisoners' preferences, and where it is necessary

in a prisoner's own interest to require that prisoner to share a cell – for example to help protect him or her from what appears to be the risk of suicide;

▶ **dormitories.** Dormitories are not a satisfactory way of accommodating prisoners. They are being phased out or redesigned with cubicles as part of the long-term refurbishment programme. This will reduce the number of places available;

▶ **population mix.** The number of places provided must take account of the geographical location of the prison population, the balance between remand and sentenced prisoners, their age, whether they are male or female, and the security conditions in which they should be held;

▶ **seasonal fluctuations.** The prison population can change quite quickly in a very short period – for example, because of the normal surge in receptions after Christmas, the number of prisoners increased by 1,300 in the first four weeks of 1991. The prison system should be able to cope with this without resort to overcrowding;

▶ **refurbishment.** It will continue to be necessary to provide for redecoration and refurbishment – as in all buildings, however modern. An allowance needs therefore to be made for a continuing programme of refurbishment which will at any one time require some of the available accommodation to be empty.

6.12 These factors have to be reflected in the Prison Service's plans to provide an estate able to operate in equilibrium without particular prisons or areas suffering from overcrowding. The Government will continue in its building and refurbishment programmes to work towards providing a prison system which can be planned and managed in this way. Subject to the sentencing decisions of the courts, and, in particular, to the effects of the Criminal Justice Act 1991, the Government considers that the prison system is in sight of providing sufficient places to match the average size of the prison population. It may be some further time before the system can cope with most contingencies without some loss of equilibrium, but that too will depend on the number of people committed to prison and the periods of time for which they have to be held.

6.13 The Government accepts that there should be greater public awareness of the degree to which there is overcrowding in any particular prison. It intends, therefore, that the Prison Service should publish in its annual report fuller information on these matters. Once the system comes into equilibrium, it will consider the possible substance of a Prison Rule and of any formal procedure to notify Parliament of any significant instance of overcrowding, as recommended in the Woolf Report. It would be necessary, however, to ensure that any formal procedure did not unintentionally appear to institutionalise a return to overcrowding.

A Code of Standards

6.14 There are, at present, a series of standards which apply to prison establishments. Standards relating to the frequency of visits, for example, are set out in Standing Orders introduced under the Prison Rules. The Government has accepted the principle of the European Prison Rules. There are full and detailed standards for the design of new prisons, which are followed, as far as possible, in refurbishment schemes. These are set out in the Prison Design Briefing System published in 1989. There are standards for changes of prisoners' clothing and bedding. Each year, the Prisons Board sets priorities for the whole of the Prison Service. Contracts between Governors and Area Managers set out the objectives and measurements of success which will apply for the coming year in each establishment. Both reflect an appreciation of the standards which should be achieved.

6.15 The Government intends to codify these various standards. They should be focused directly on the service to be provided for prisoners. They should cover the standard of accommodation, such as cell space, heating and lighting; the basic necessities of life, such as the provision of food and clothing and hygiene arrangements; and the access which prisoners should have to a range of regime facilities, including visits and other contacts with families and friends.

6.16 The standards would be set at the level necessary for the Prison Service to meet the obligations described in Chapter 1. It follows that the level should be such as to provide humane and decent conditions which allow prisoners to maintain their self-respect and some hope for a better future.

6.17 The principal aim of the standards would be to set clear targets which all establishments would in time be expected to meet; and against which the provisions in any particular establishment could be judged. They would, therefore, provide a valuable means for enhancing the management of the Prison Service and its ability to deliver services to prisoners. They would provide an objective framework within which the annual contracts between Area Managers and Governors could be drawn up. They would also help to determine priorities for the allocation of resources between establishments.

6.18 Progress towards meeting the standards in any particular prison would be dependent on the efficiency of management and the skill of staff in identifying and delivering the priorities; and on the country's ability to afford any additional resources necessary to achieve an improvement. The time taken to meet the standards would depend also on the level at which they were set.

6.19 The Prison Service has begun work on preparing such standards. In taking forward this work, it will consult the unions, outside organisations and prisoners. It will be necessary to consider not only the right level for each standard but also their number and complexity, the ground they should cover, and whether to have a single set of standards for all establishments, or to produce variations according to the type of establishment or the legal status of the prisoner.

6.20 In the course of this work, the Government will consider whether a system of certificates of accreditation is the best way of signifying when the standards have been met, as the Woolf Report recommended. The Government is sympathetic to the notion that when any specific standard is met, a certificate might be given to the establishment by the Area Manager and that, when all standards have been met in any prison, the Home Secretary might

grant that prison accredited status on the recommendation of the Chief Inspector. Once the standards were achieved, continued compliance might be monitored by the Board of Visitors and by Her Majesty's Chief Inspector during the course of his inspections.

6.21 The Government agrees with the Woolf Report that questions relating to enshrining the standards in the Prison Rules, and to their enforceability, should be considered when the standards can be met consistently in all establishments. It would be necessary also to review the standards from time to time to ensure that they continue to meet the public's expectations of the Prison Service.

6.22 Two further issues relating to standards in prison reflect the Government's view that greater restrictions should not be placed on a prisoner than are a necessary consequence of the decision of the courts to commit the person to custody. They relate to health services and to prisoners' clothing.

Health

6.23 Prisoners should expect the same standards of health care as those provided by the National Health Service. The prison regime must enable health care to be delivered effectively. The way the service is delivered must take account of the fact that these patients are also prisoners who, for the most part, must be held in custody while they are being treated. It must recognise also that the nature of the physical and psychological ailments presented by prisoners is not the same as that found in the average general practitioner's practice.

6.24 An Efficiency Scrutiny conducted in

1990 proposed substantial reform of the Prison Medical Service. The general thrust of the 83 detailed recommendations contained in the Scrutiny was that the Prison Medical Service should become a Prison Health Service much more closely aligned to the National Health Service; that it should reflect National Health Service developments in health promotion and the prevention of illness; and in particular that the Service should purchase under contract from the National Health Service (or other providers) the full range of health care services required.

6.25 The scrutineers found, as others have found before them, that the Prison Medical Service should continue to be managed as part of the Prison Service as a whole, but that much closer association with the National Health Service would be beneficial. The Government accepts this finding and welcomes the opportunity which the Scrutiny presents for moving closer to the National Health Service. The Government has already accepted in principle some of the key recommendations of the Scrutiny Report, in particular that:

▶ the role of the Prison Medical Service should be widened to that of a Prison Health Service;

▶ a Health Advisory Committee should be appointed to advise on health care;

▶ all prison establishments should undertake medical audit;

▶ the provision made through the Prison Health Service should relate as closely as possible to the identified needs of prisoners;

▶ the medical management of the Prison

Health Service should be improved;

▶ the management of the Prison Health Service should be more fully integrated into the management of the Prison Service.

6.26 The Prison Service will be taking forward these proposals and the consideration of the remaining recommendations in close consultation with the Department of Health and the National Health Service over the next 12 months. Detailed consideration must be given to the resource implications and to the practical issues for both the Prison Service's staff and the National Health Service in implementing the necessary changes. Throughout this work, the Government's continuing commitment will be to achieve a better health service for all prisoners.

Clothing

6.27 It has long been the practice that male convicted prisoners should wear prison issue clothing. This does not apply to female prisoners, nor to unconvicted prisoners.

6.28 Many aspects of prison life are geared to this practice. The Prison Service laundries – which provide employment for nearly 1,000 prisoners – are organised to wash Prison Service clothing rather than to provide an individual service for the clothes brought in by each prisoner. Prison Service industries make most of the clothing and footwear worn in prisons – providing employment for some 4,000 prisoners. Prison issue clothing can assist in distinguishing between prisoners and others – particularly on visits – and can make an abscond or escape more difficult. It also ensures that prisoners in workshops wear clothing which protects their health and safety.

6.29 Prison clothing, however, does not easily make allowances for the individuality of each prisoner; nor is it conducive to allowing prisoners to exercise greater choice and responsibility. Prisoners can feel more responsible for their own lives if they have more choice about what to wear and if they know they can be held accountable for keeping their clothes in reasonable condition. The Prison Service has sought to tackle this latter issue by introducing personal kit systems for longer term sentenced prisoners. Requirements for changing prisoners' clothing are set out in the Governor's contract with the Area Manager. There is currently a major programme to increase the choice and quantity of underwear, and to improve the design of footwear.

6.30 The Government intends, however, to go further in providing opportunities for convicted male prisoners to exercise responsibility for and choice in what they wear. Accordingly, the Government aims progressively to allow these prisoners to wear their own clothes, if they so wish. The achievement of this objective must allow for practical considerations, such as washing and laundering arrangements, health and safety factors and the likely effect on the availability of work for prisoners. These matters will be assessed in the light of experience with pilot schemes. The Prison Service has already introduced a pilot scheme at Belmarsh prison, London, which, since its opening in April 1991, has enabled all prisoners to wear their own clothes. Pilot schemes will be introduced in two other establishments. The Prison Service will consider in the course of the pilot schemes the scope for permitting prisoners to wear specified items of their own clothing, in particular, underwear, socks and shoes, in advance of extending the arrangements to prisoners' outerwear.

6.31 The extent of these provisions and the pace at which they can be introduced will depend on the experience of the pilot schemes; on finding suitable alternative work for prisoners; and on identifying acceptable arrangements for laundering prisoners' own clothes. The changes are therefore likely to be phased and will take some years to implement in full.

Food

6.32 The Prison Service recognises the central importance which the quality and type of food – and the way it is served – can play in the life of prisoners. Nutritious food of reasonable quality, well presented and served, can significantly raise the morale of prisoners, and therefore their readiness to contribute to and co-operate in the life and opportunities of the prison. Provisional information from the National Prison Survey (1) suggests that prisoners give a high priority to having better food.

6.33 The Prison Service has done much in recent years to improve the quality, type and choice of food served in prisons:

▶ it has invested nearly £11m on the renovation of prison kitchens in the last two years;

▶ it plans to spend a further £56.5m over this and the next two years;

▶ it has introduced National Vocational Qualifications for prisoners working in kitchens;

▶ it has introduced a choice of meals in many prisons, for example at Cardiff and Kirkham prisons, and it has provided special diets for vegetarians, vegans and to reflect religious and ethnic requirements;

▶ it reviewed the dietary scales in 1990 and introduced changes to give caterers more discretion in the use of their budgets and to improve the nutritional balance of the diet;

▶ it has commissioned a research project which is being undertaken by the University of Surrey to review all aspects of the provision of food in establishments, including nutritional quality, catering efficiency and its acceptability to prisoners, including those in the main religious and ethnic groups. The project started at the beginning of this year.

6.34 For the future, the Prison Service will:

▶ **prepare a new catering strategy for the Prison Service.** This will identify the scope for giving greater budgetary discretion to caterers. Implementation will take account of the findings of the University of Surrey's research project;

▶ **introduce the option of allowing prisoners to eat in association** and out of their cells where this is not done already and where the space, security and staffing implications will allow it;

▶ **consider ways of enabling prisoners to eat at more social hours,** both at mid-day and in the early evening, taking account of the scope for re-arranging staff rotas and of any consequent staffing implications.

Conclusion

6.35 Taken together, the proposals in this Chapter will provide an objective structure in which to continue the improvements which have already been made to standards in prisons. They establish also clear priorities: to end slopping out by December 1994; and to work progressively towards the end of overcrowding within the prison system. The proposals recognise the individuality and humanity of prisoners and the obligation to provide prisoners with decent as well as secure conditions.

Notes

(1) The National Prison Survey was conducted by the Office of Population Censuses and Surveys between January and March 1991. It was commissioned on behalf of the Prison Service by the Home Office Research and Planning Unit. The analysis of its results will be completed later this year.

1 Training in computer skills – HMRC Low Newton

2 Mother and baby unit – HMP Holloway

3 Construction and industry training – HMYOI Onley

4 The dairy – HMP Stocken

5 Pre-release training – HMP Birmingham

6 Visits area – HMP Stocken

7 Prisoners' cardphone – HMP Holloway

8 HIV/AIDS and drug misuse – information for prisoners and staff

Introduction

7.1   This Chapter sets out the Government's plans for ensuring that prisoners spend their time in active, demanding and rewarding ways relevant to their needs and to the reasons why they are in prison. A full and properly prepared routine will make a major contribution to a stable prison system and to the way prisoners may be expected to approach their time in prison. Close co-operation from and co-ordination with statutory and voluntary agencies in the community are essential in providing well-rounded programmes linked to a prisoner's plan after release. Programmes must give sentenced prisoners every opportunity to acquire the skills and resolve necessary not to commit further crimes. These objectives will be achieved only if the programmes are carefully planned and if they are introduced in a way which demonstrates a constructive relationship between prisoners and those who work with them.

Purpose of Programmes

7.2   Prison programmes should serve the following purposes. They should:

▷   help prisoners stay mentally alert and physically fit and so prevent damaging inactivity and inertia;

▷   ensure prisoners contribute to the life and upkeep of the prison;

▷   improve prisoners' educational levels and technical skills; give them opportunities for self advancement and self fulfilment; challenge sentenced prisoners about their criminal behaviour – so that they leave prison better adjusted, less likely to be bitter about their experiences, and more likely to lead constructive and law-abiding lives;

▷   assist unconvicted prisoners additionally to identify any factors which would enable a court to release them on bail; to enable them to prepare for their trials and to protect their livelihood, property and other interests; and enable them to live a life in prison consistent with their unconvicted status;

▷   give prisoners reasonable opportunities to maintain links with their families and an interest in and knowledge of the world outside prison;

▷   give prisoners some responsibility and choice over the way they spend their time;

▷   show that the Prison Service respects the individuality and humanity of prisoners.

Policy Objectives: Convicted and Unconvicted Prisoners

7.3   These objectives apply in different ways and to different extents for convicted prisoners and for unconvicted prisoners on remand. The Woolf Report accepted that, for convicted prisoners, they were encapsulated in the Prison Service's Statement of Purpose referred to in Chapter 1:

"Her Majesty's Prison Service serves the public by keeping in custody those committed by the courts.

Our duty is to look after them with humanity and to help them lead law-abiding and useful lives in custody and after release."

7.4 The value of a statement such as this is that it applies to all the tasks of the Prison Service, and it is sufficiently succinct to be easily assimilated by staff, prisoners, visitors to the prison and by the general public. In the Government's view, it would not make for a Service working together for a common purpose if the Prison Service were to replace this with separate statements of purposes relating more narrowly to its individual tasks and policies, or to the main categories of prisoners for which it provides. The Government considers that the existing Statement of Purpose is broadly relevant to all aspects of the Prison Service's work and should remain in its present succinct form. In coming to this conclusion, the Government has noted the Woolf Report's conclusion that there is nothing in the language of the Statement of Purpose which cannot be applied to remand prisoners.

7.5 The Government accepts, however, that the Statement of Purpose is not, by itself, a full or sufficient statement of the Prison Service's role in respect of unconvicted prisoners. The Government accepts that there should be a separate statement for them which reinforces the Prison Service's commitment to recognising their particular legal status and the particular requirements which follow from that status. The Government has, therefore, decided:

▶ **that there will be a separate statement for unconvicted prisoners.** This will be a short statement of principle, publicly available, reflecting the considerations for unconvicted prisoners identified in the Woolf Report;

▶ **that the statements of tasks and functions for establishments holding unconvicted prisoners will**

be reviewed and if necessary amended to ensure that they adequately reflect the separate status of these prisoners. These statements form the basis of the contracts which are drawn up between Governors and Area Managers;

▶ **that the facilities available in establishments holding unconvicted prisoners will be reflected in the statement of facilities for prisoners.** These statements are referred to later in this Chapter;

▶ **that the Prison Rules will be substantially revised so that separate rules would apply to unconvicted prisoners held on remand.**

7.6 The objectives which the Prison Service sets itself for the treatment of both convicted and unconvicted prisoners must be reflected in the way they are treated and in the programmes which are provided for them. This Chapter identifies the ways in which these objectives will be realised.

Present Provision

7.7 The Prison Service has concentrated in recent years on monitoring the overall delivery of programmes to prisoners and on introducing regime initiatives in particular prisons.

7.8 There have been some significant improvements in the way prisoners spend their time in prison. In some prisons, particularly open and training prisons, prisoners are able to spend a large amount of the working day and early evening out of their cells in organised and less formal activities. The average number of hours prisoners spent out of their cells on organised activities increased to over 22 hours a week in 1990/91 – an improvement of nearly 7% on the previous year. They are set out by type of establishment in Table 1.

Table 1		
Number of hours each week spent by prisoners in organised activities (work, education, chaplaincy classes, PE, induction)		
Type of	*Performance*	
establishment	*1989/90*	*1990/91*
Dispersal	21.82	20.31
Other Category B (male)	21.71	22.30
Category C (male)	26.85	26.95
Category D (male)	34.64	37.59
Remand (male)	12.60	11.87
Local (male)	13.61	15.47
YOI Closed (male)	22.67	22.29
YOI Open (male)	35.94	36.98
YOI D/C (male)	35.61	35.41
Female (training)	29.21	30.76
Female (local/remand)	17.89	22.91
OVERALL	**20.87**	**22.29**

Note: YOI D/C = Young offender institution direct committal. These establishments (previously detention centres) receive young offenders direct from the courts.

7.9 Many of these organised activities will have taken place during the working week. These figures take no account of the time spent on association, visits, or other such activities which, in many cases, would considerably

increase the amount of time a prisoner is able to spend out of the cell. The figures for 1990/91 are likely to be lower than they would otherwise have been because of the disruption caused during and following the disturbances in April 1990. Nevertheless, the figures suggest a clear need for improvement in the provision of organised activities in particular types of establishment, particularly remand centres and local prisons. Overall, they suggest a level of provision which is significantly less than the Government believes desirable.

7.10 There have nevertheless been considerable increases in the provision of key activities. For example, the number of student education hours increased from 5.56 million hours in 1987/88 to 7.75 million hours in 1989/90. The number of prisoner hours of physical education increased from 5.07 million hours to 5.22 million hours over the same period. The average number of hours worked each week by prisoners in workshops increased from 19.4 hours to 21.7 hours between 1987 and 1990. Profiles of the ways occupied prisoners were spending their day in prison establishments in March 1991 are given in Figure 1 overleaf. These profiles do not reflect time spent in cell, or time out of cell on such activities as association, PE or visits.

7.11 The Prison Service intends to improve its monitoring systems so that:

▶ it is able to chart more accurately progress towards increasing the time prisoners spend out of their cells;

▶ the monitoring reports provide some reflection of the quality of provision;

▶ in time, the experiences of individual prisoners can be monitored.

Figure 1 Profile of inmate occupation – March 1991

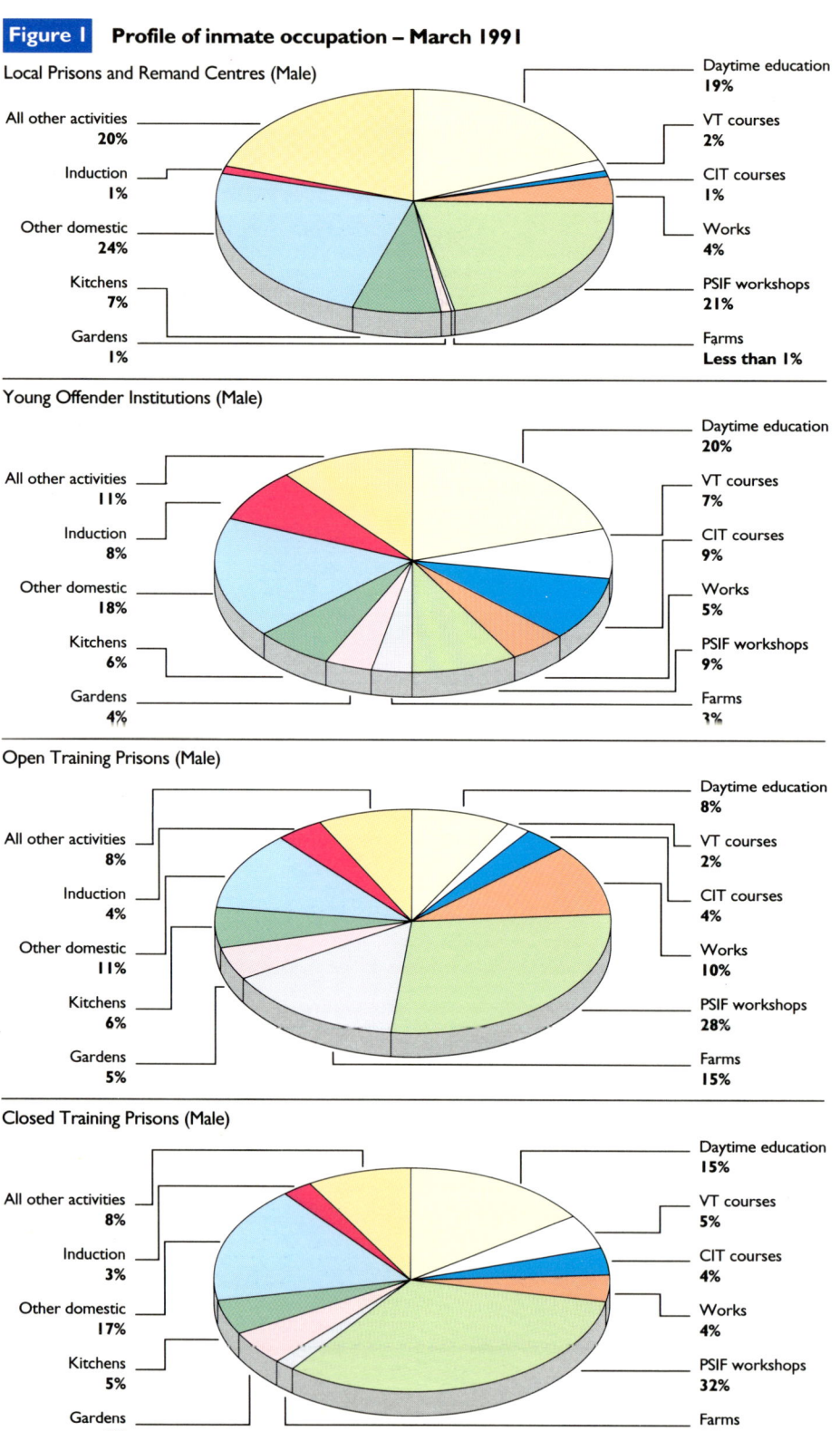

Local Prisons and Remand Centres (Male)

All other activities 20%
Induction 1%
Other domestic 24%
Kitchens 7%
Gardens 1%

Daytime education 19%
VT courses 2%
CIT courses 1%
Works 4%
PSIF workshops 21%
Farms Less than 1%

Young Offender Institutions (Male)

All other activities 11%
Induction 8%
Other domestic 18%
Kitchens 6%
Gardens 4%

Daytime education 20%
VT courses 7%
CIT courses 9%
Works 5%
PSIF workshops 9%
Farms 3%

Open Training Prisons (Male)

All other activities 8%
Induction 4%
Other domestic 11%
Kitchens 6%
Gardens 5%

Daytime education 8%
VT courses 2%
CIT courses 4%
Works 10%
PSIF workshops 28%
Farms 15%

Closed Training Prisons (Male)

All other activities 8%
Induction 3%
Other domestic 17%
Kitchens 5%
Gardens 5%

Daytime education 15%
VT courses 5%
CIT courses 4%
Works 4%
PSIF workshops 32%
Farms 2%

Local Prisons and Remand Centres (Female)

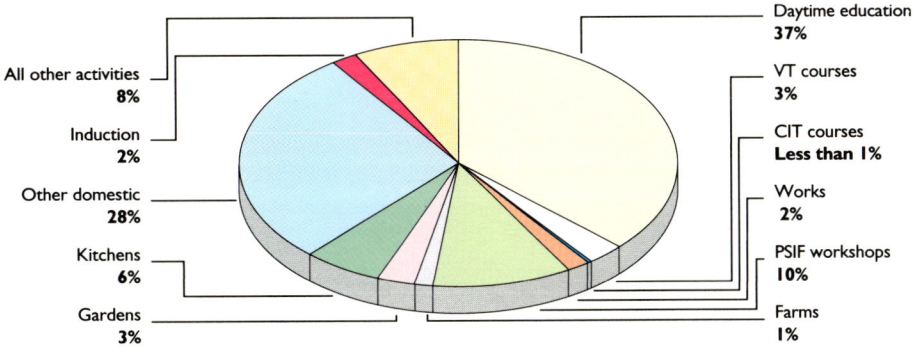

All other activities
8%

Induction
2%

Other domestic
28%

Kitchens
6%

Gardens
3%

Daytime education
37%

VT courses
3%

CIT courses
Less than 1%

Works
2%

PSIF workshops
10%

Farms
1%

Training Establishments (Female)

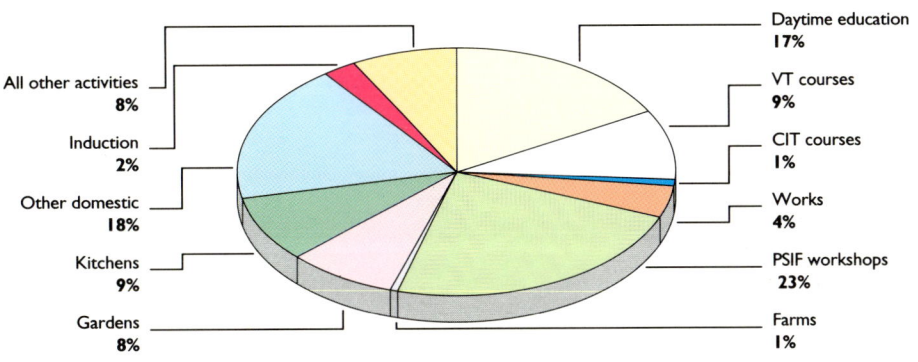

All other activities
8%

Induction
2%

Other domestic
18%

Kitchens
9%

Gardens
8%

Daytime education
17%

VT courses
9%

CIT courses
1%

Works
4%

PSIF workshops
23%

Farms
1%

All Establishments

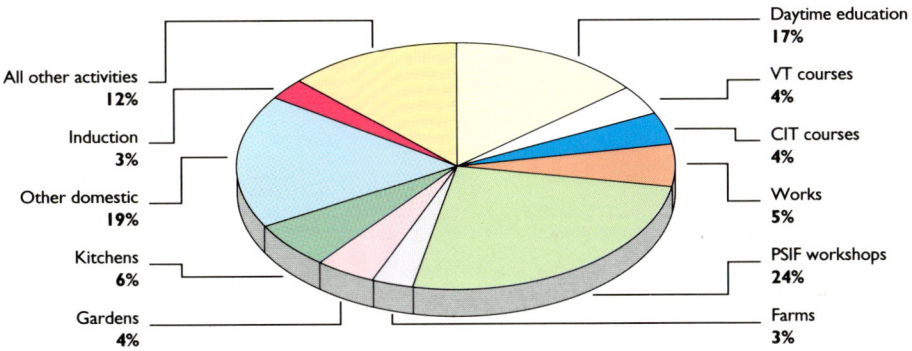

All other activities
12%

Induction
3%

Other domestic
19%

Kitchens
6%

Gardens
4%

Daytime education
17%

VT courses
4%

CIT courses
4%

Works
5%

PSIF workshops
24%

Farms
3%

Note: PSIF - Prison Service Industries and Farms   CIT - Construction and Industry Training   VT - Vocational Training

7.12 Many individual prisons have developed new and increased regime opportunities. Some are referred to in the published annual reports on the work of the Prison Service. The following is a small sample of what is currently being achieved:

▶ Low Newton remand centre provides modular education courses allowing its population of mainly unconvicted prisoners to pursue courses in such subjects as numeracy, communication skills, creative writing, health and substance misuse;

▶ for the last two years, the Education Officer at Littlehey Category C prison for adult male prisoners has organised a summer school for prisoners not normally involved in education classes. It is based on art and craft workshops;

▶ over the last three years, Thorn Cross young offender institution has established a PE Vocational Training Course in co-operation with Wigan College of Technology. Success rates have been high;

▶ a recently discharged prisoner from Drake Hall women's prison has demonstrated how integrated programmes can lead to successful rehabilitation. Having completed a painting and decorating course, she joined an officer-led pre-release course which included an input on small businesses from Stafford Enterprise. On discharge, she applied successfully for a grant and runs a thriving decorating business.

7.13 There is still a very long way to go before these examples are the common experience of all prisoners. Although some establishments have managed to keep workshops and farms operating with the number of inmates for which they had budgeted, and for a reasonable length working day, many others have operated at well under full capacity, and for hours which fall well short of a normal working day outside prison. In particular, remand prisoners and those in local prisons generally have the most restricted opportunities. They need particular attention in the years ahead.

An Active Day

7.14 The Government believes that programmes should aim to provide an active day for all prisoners during the week and at weekends. The amount of time a prisoner is able to spend out of his or her cell on constructive activities is affected by the way the prison is managed, the staff available, the way they are deployed and the nature and extent of the facilities available. The Government intends that improvements should be made progressively in all these areas. The completion of the corporate objectives exercise should contribute to improving the management of the available resources and identify what might be achieved if additional resources were available.

Induction, Regimes and Sentence Planning

7.15 The Prison Service has already made progress in identifying the elements which should make up the regimes for each of the groups of prisoners in its care, and in developing a strategy for planning programmes with prisoners.

7.16 In particular it has:

▶ provided induction programmes in a number of training establishments. These are usually conducted by prison officers, but with the assistance of others, including the probation service and the chaplaincy. The programme at Camp Hill prison, for example, lasts for ten days and covers such areas as entitlements to letters and visits, facilities available in the prison, educational testing, probation and throughcare;

▶ established the regimes which should apply in young offender institutions. These are set out in some detail in an Instruction issued in September 1988;

▶ provided sentence plans for those in young offender institutions;

▶ provided sentence plans for most life sentence prisoners;

▶ established in September 1990 a new Directorate of Inmate Programmes with specific responsibilities for promoting improved prison regimes.

7.17 The Prison Service intends to build on and extend this work. It aims to provide for all prisoners more effective induction arrangements and a greater assurance of adequate and predictable regimes which relate to all aspects of their daily lives in prison and to their obligations on release. In particular, the Prison Service will:

▶ **review the reception and induction arrangements for prisoners.** This review will be completed by the end of 1991. It will help to identify the best way of providing prisoners with the information

and support they need during their early days in prison and ensure that staff recognise and start to tackle any immediate problems which need to be resolved. The review will include consideration of the circumstances in which screening for suicide risk takes place;

▶ **prepare comprehensive guidance on regimes for establishments holding women prisoners.** The guidance will identify the ways in which regimes for women can meet their particular needs. The Prison Service will take account of the views expressed by the Women's National Commission in their report "Women and Prison" (1) published in April 1991;

▶ **prepare a model regime for local prisons and remand centres, taking particular account of the needs of unconvicted prisoners.** The aim is to consult widely within the Prison Service and among interested outside bodies before issuing the guidance to Governors next year. This guidance will be relevant to the work on standards discussed in the previous Chapter;

▶ **prepare or revise guidance on regimes in other establishments;**

▶ **encourage establishments to continue to develop effective pre-release courses involving prison officers and outside voluntary and other agencies.** Such courses provide valuable practical assistance to prisoners and useful counselling on such matters as alcohol and drug misuse;

▶ **help prepare national standards for**

probation service supervision of prisoners during their time in prison and after release. These standards will be issued on implementation of the Criminal Justice Act 1991. They will cover the role of the probation officer working in prison and the role during the custodial part of the sentence of the probation officer from the prisoner's home area. They will cover also the ways in which supervision during the community part of the sentence is to be carried out. The aim will be to ensure continuity in the programme of work undertaken by and with the prisoner in custody and when under supervision in the community.

7.18 This work will be taken forward in concert with work on sentence planning. Sentence plans can ensure that the best use is made of a prisoner's time in prison and provide an opportunity to keep under review his or her progress during the sentence. They will become increasingly important with the implementation of the Criminal Justice Act 1991 which provides that, for sentences of one year or more, supervision should continue as part of the sentence following release from prison. This will require the time in prison to be co-ordinated and consistent with the period under supervision. This can best be achieved through a sentence plan which takes account of both parts of the sentence, prepared in consultation with the probation service.

7.19 There are already well developed sentence planning arrangements, for example, at adult male prisons at Full Sutton, Morton Hall and North Sea Camp, and at the women's prison at Drake Hall. These and other establishments provide a sound foundation on which to build.

In particular, the Government will:

▶ **introduce and improve sentence plans for all life sentence prisoners.** The Government is considering introducing a more structured plan centred on offending behaviour and setting programme objectives which will determine progress towards release;

▶ **introduce in 1992 sentence plans for Category A prisoners and for sex offenders;**

▶ **move towards providing sentence plans for all prisoners serving substantial sentences as resources allow.** Priority will be given to prisoners sentenced to imprisonment for four years or more since the release of such prisoners under supervision is discretionary under the provisions of the Criminal Justice Act 1991. In the longer term, the aim will be to prepare a suitable form of sentence plan for all prisoners other than those who will be in custody for only a short time.

Delivery of Regimes

7.20 The involvement of prisoners in the management of their time provides an important additional dimension to the value of the activities which they undertake. Prison management may ultimately require a convicted prisoner to take part in work or otherwise require a prisoner to undertake some particular duty or activity. But the aims should be to ensure that each prisoner understands the nature of the routine and has an element of choice in some, at least, of the activities in which he or she participates. The Government therefore intends that:

▶ **the personal officer scheme should be extended to a wider range of prisoners.** These schemes at present apply in young offender institutions and at some adult prisons – there are, for example, well-developed arrangements at Swinfen Hall young offender institution and at Acklington prison for adult prisoners. In such schemes, a prison officer is assigned to each prisoner – one officer will be the personal officer for a number of prisoners. The appointed officer acts as the prisoner's first point of contact. Experience has shown that this system improves relationships between prisoners and staff and enhances the quality of the prison officer's job. The Prison Service intends to expand the scheme or analogous schemes on a phased basis and as resources allow, so that their value, including their value to those serving short sentences and those on remand, can be assessed;

▶ **prisoners should, wherever possible, be given the reasons for decisions which affect them.** This will influence the way information is communicated between headquarters and establishments, and within the management structure of the prison. Staff need to be given clear reasons, as well as prisoners;

▶ **there should be moves towards greater openness in discussions with prisoners about the conduct of their sentences.** This should start with the preparation and periodic review of sentence plans and, for longer term and life sentence prisoners, might move towards more open reporting on progress and the giving of reasons for decisions by the Parole Board and Ministers when cases are reviewed. Openness will be a part of the new arrangements under the Criminal Justice Act 1991 for the review and release of prisoners;

▶ **there should be increased consultation with prisoners on general issues which affect their daily lives.** This will be developed at all levels. On behalf of the Prison Service, the Home Office Research and Planning Unit has commissioned the Office of Population Censuses and Surveys to undertake a National Prison Survey involving interviewing 10% of all prisoners (and 20% of female prisoners) in every prison establishment. Some of the preliminary findings have already been referred to in this White Paper. A consultation document prepared in March 1991 on possible changes to the disciplinary system in the light of the Woolf Report was placed in every prison library and prisoners were invited to respond. Some prisons already provide opportunities for prisoners to have regular meetings with the Governor or at wing level or on particular matters, such as food. The Prison Service will consider how these initiatives can be developed and more widely used at all levels in the Service;

▶ **an information pack, prepared jointly by the Prison Service and the Prison Reform Trust, should be available shortly to all prisoners.** The pack provides basic information, clearly expressed, about the various regulations and procedures which apply to life in prison;

▶ **statements of facilities for and what is expected of prisoners – prisoner compacts – should be introduced, initially on a pilot basis, in selected prison establishments.** The pilot projects would take account of work already undertaken at Blantyre House and Latchmere prisons. They would be a form of the prisoner's "compact" recommended in the Woolf Report. They would complement any sentence plan prepared for the prisoner. They would set out the facilities which were available to the prisoner; the opportunities and choices he or she would have; and what was expected in return. The statements would be signed by the Governor or the Governor's representative and the prisoner would be given the opportunity to sign as well. The statements would be factual rather than aspirational: they would reflect current provision. If the prisoner's expectations were not met, then the statement would provide a basis for finding out the reason and for deciding whether to make a complaint through the grievance procedure. It would also provide a framework within which changes and developments could be explained to a prisoner. The Prison Service will consult widely within and outside the Service, and among prisoners, on the form the statement might take. The purpose of the pilot scheme would be to identify what might usefully be incorporated in the statements and any consequent resource implications. The pace of introduction would depend on the outcome of the pilot schemes.

Nature of Programmes

7.21 Programmes must take account of the requirements of the prison, the resources which are available, and the need to provide constructive opportunities for prisoners. The aim must be to produce as full a range of activities and opportunities as the available resources will allow. Programmes must allow for work, and, at the appropriate time, access to education and training, as well as PE, opportunities for religious observance, association and exercise. They must make due allowance for visits and for any other activities or groups in which the prisoner may need to be involved.

7.22 Work has a central role in the prison regime. It ensures that convicted prisoners contribute to the cost of their upkeep by helping with the running and maintenance of the prison and by providing goods and services in prison industries and on prison farms. The prison day needs to be arranged to make best and fullest use of the work available. Workshops allow industrial skills to be practised; farm work offers externally recognised qualifications. The pace and type of work should be closer to work in the community. Experience of regular work in prison can be a useful preparation for seeking a job on release. To these ends, the Prison Service intends:

▶ **to improve the quality of work by prison workshops gaining accreditation to British Standard 5750** (2);

▶ **to consider introducing pilot schemes increasing the involvement of private employers,** so as to extend the range of work available;

▶ **to give further opportunities for obtaining recognised qualifications** through work place training, including National Vocational Qualifications;

▶ **to introduce a new workshop management information system for Governors** so as to increase the information they have about the individual performances of workshops and so improve their management of work in their establishments;

▶ **to continue to encourage Governors to identify potential local sources of work for their workshops** and to ensure that headquarters follow up such leads within 24 hours of receiving the information from Governors.

7.23 Education is an essential part of the opportunities which must be provided in a prison. Many prisoners have inadequate educational and social skills. The first priority for the education programme must be to identify and provide help for those prisoners who have difficulty reading or writing, and who are unable to do simple arithmetic. Without such basic skills, the prospects for prisoners to live fulfilling and law-abiding lives on release will be much diminished. There should be opportunities to develop artistic and other skills so as to give prisoners a sense of personal achievement and self-respect. Education programmes should provide opportunities for prisoners to acquire qualifications which could be useful in the prison's work programmes and which will improve their prospects on release. To fulfil their potential, these programmes must be well managed and integrated with the rest of the regime and with the prisoner's plans on release.

7.24 National Vocational Qualifications are a central element in achieving these objectives. The Prison Service intends considerably to extend access to these qualifications. It recently appointed a full-time co-ordinator for National Vocational Qualifications, assisted by five developmental officers. Their task will be to encourage the introduction of these qualifications in all establishments across a wide range of activities, including training and work programmes. In addition, the Prison Service intends to improve the effectiveness of its provision by:

▶ **increasing the use of modular education courses for remand and short sentenced prisoners;**

▶ **introducing written agreements – a form of "compact" – between each establishment and the college of further education responsible for delivering the service.** These would define their respective roles and responsibilities and so provide clear lines of accountability;

▶ **introducing a common method for evaluating the effectiveness of the education provision in each establishment.**

7.25 The relationship between work, education and training is central in determining the nature of regimes in prison. (A breakdown of the time spent on different activities by occupied inmates in the first quarter of 1991 is shown in Figure 2 overleaf.) In establishing the relationship, the Government has two objectives:

▷ **a balanced regime.** The Prison Service should aim to provide as wide a range of opportunities in its programmes as possible. It is not an industrial enterprise. It is not an educational institution. It is not a training body. But each of these activities – and others – is required to meet the obligations of the Prison Service described in Chapter 1. The activities must be relevant to the prisoner on release and create as normal a working life as possible. It follows that work should have a central place in the life of the prison and that convicted prisoners should normally be expected to work. Education should continue to be voluntary (except for juveniles). Daytime education should focus on providing basic education and skills and on encouraging and providing vocational training. Prisoners in full-time education should be enabled wherever possible to complete their courses. Other education activities must not be seen as alternatives to these provisions or to participating in available work;

▷ **a responsive regime.** The programmes should be developed to meet the requirements of prisoners – in terms of their education and training needs and of their needs for any particular programmes to address their offending. Not all prisoners will require such programmes, but some prisoners will need to be given these opportunities at particular stages in their sentences. The precise balance will be a matter for their sentence plans.

7.26 The Prison Service is currently reviewing the balance required of regimes in the light of these objectives, taking into account the costs of each of the different activities. The aim will be to make full use of the opportunities which can be offered as overcrowding reduces and as new and refurbished facilities become available, as well as to identify any resource implications associated with more substantial regime improvements. The intention, in consultation with Governors, is to establish guidelines for Governors on the provision of regimes in their prisons. These guidelines will consider which activities should be given priority during the working day, and which could be used to enrich programmes during the evenings and at weekends.

Pay and Facilities

7.27 Prisoners cannot expect to receive an income which is commensurate in level and range with that received by people in the community. Equally, prisoners cannot be expected to earn enough to keep themselves or to meet their responsibilities outside. In 1989/90 it cost on average £554 a week to keep a prisoner in a high security dispersal prison; and on average £218 a week to keep a prisoner in an open prison. Very few prisoners would be able to earn the cost of their keep through their own work. Pay should be set at levels which reward effort, which provide incentives and which recognise the value of the prisoner's contribution to the life of the establishment.

7.28 Present pay levels are intended:

▷ to enable prisoners to buy everyday personal items – for example tobacco, toiletries, confectionery;

▷ to allow prisoners to meet the cost of maintaining links with the outside world – traditionally through correspondence and now, increasingly, through the telephone;

Figure 2   **Proportion of time spent on different activities by occupied inmates-January to March 1991**

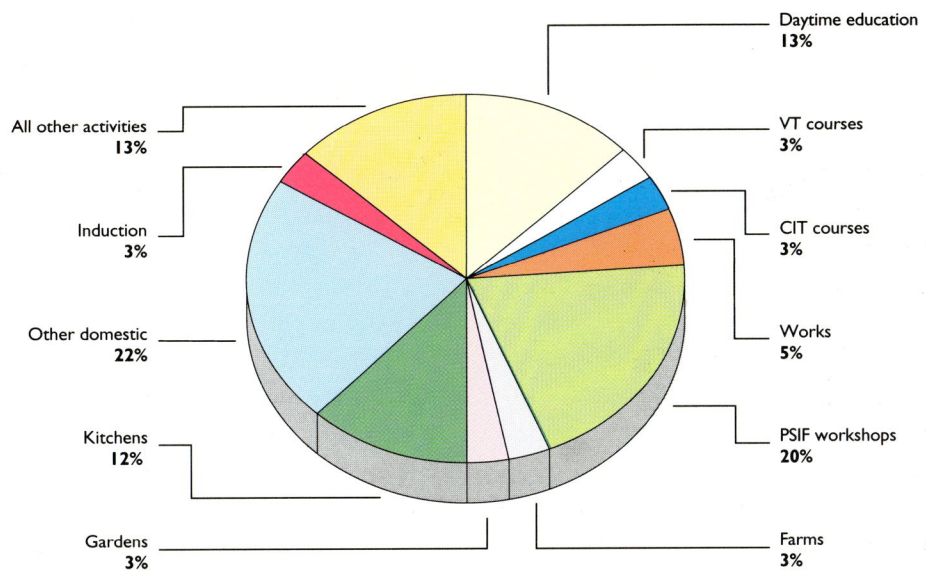

Daytime education 13%
VT courses 3%
CIT courses 3%
Works 5%
PSIF workshops 20%
Farms 3%
Gardens 3%
Kitchens 12%
Other domestic 22%
Induction 3%
All other activities 13%

Note: PSIF - Prison Service Industries and Farms   CIT - Construction and Industry Training   VT - Vocational Training

▷ to relieve, at least to some extent, the burden on the families of those prisoners who send them cash for such requirements;

▷ to give prisoners an opportunity to make choices and to exert some responsibility for their lives.

7.29 The basic pay levels were uprated in April 1991. They now range from £1.90 for unemployed prisoners to £6.40 a week for the employed. Some prisoners may earn more than the basic levels by overtime working. During the April uprating, the levels were made consistent so that unconvicted prisoners who elect to work are able to earn the same pay as convicted prisoners. A basic "retirement" pay was also introduced for prisoners who have passed normal working age.

7.30 In the coming years the Government would wish to see increased pay levels. The initial aim would be to introduce a system which, when resources allowed, would provide an average weekly wage of about £8, as the Woolf Report proposed. The particular level at which each prisoner was paid would depend on performance. Governors would be given greater discretion in the way pay was apportioned in their establishments so that pay levels could be geared to providing the incentives necessary to help meet the objectives and targets in each prison.

7.31 The Government accepts the Woolf Report's view that the remuneration for those undertaking education should not be set at levels which discourage prisoners from receiving the education they need. They should reflect effort and achievement. But the Government would wish to provide higher payments to those in work to reward productivity, particularly where it may generate extra revenue or savings to offset the higher pay.

7.32 The Prison Service is therefore exploring the possibility of linking the additional expenditure required to meet the cost of substantially increased pay levels to the revenue generated by output from productive work, or to the offsetting savings made in the cost of imprisonment. If it were possible in the longer term to establish cost-effective ways of providing substantial increases in pay levels, the Government would expect prisoners to contribute to their maintenance in the establishment; and to the maintenance of their families and dependents outside. It would also be open to prisoners to contribute to victim support schemes.

7.33 The Prison Service has reviewed the facilities available to prisoners at present set out in Standing Order 4. It intends shortly to issue a revised standing order which will, as proposed in the Woolf Report, identify those facilities to which a prisoner can normally expect to have access. In the longer term, the Prison Service aims to extend the facilities available to be able to mark better a prisoner's progress through his or her time in prison.

7.34 The Government has considered whether among these facilities it should be possible for prisoners to have televisions in their cells or rooms. This is now the common practice in many other prison systems. It is clear from the preliminary results of the National Prison Survey (3) that such a development would be seen as a high priority by many prisoners. Prisoners are at present able to have radios and record or cassette players and there is no significant point of principle which should prevent their having a television. In some prisons there have been experiments with battery operated television sets. Television should not, however, be used as a substitute for prisoners spending an active day out of their cells. Any arrangements for the use of television would need to make this clear. There are also licensing considerations. To help determine whether and under what conditions there might be opportunities for television in cells, the Prison Service will be conducting carefully monitored experiments in a small number of prisons.

Family Links

7.35 Visits and home leave provide valuable opportunities for prisoners to maintain links with their families and friends; and, at the end of their sentences, to start to re-establish themselves in the community. They are key elements in meeting the Prison Service's obligations to those in its care. The preliminary results of the National Prison Survey (3) suggest that a significant proportion of prisoners preparing for their release see home leave as particularly valuable. Letters and the use of telephones are also important ways of maintaining regular contact with the outside world. All are equally important for prisoners' families: the Prison Service has a duty also to take into account their interests and concerns.

7.36 The Home Secretary announced on 25 February 1991, on publication of the Woolf Report, an extensive programme of reform. That programme involved:

▶ **increasing the level of visits.** Adult convicted prisoners may now receive two visits every four weeks, and the length of these visits has been extended. Unconvicted prisoners should, wherever practicable, receive three one-hour visits a week;

▶ **extending financially assisted visits.** Financial assistance is now available for the initial reception visit to an unconvicted prisoner. Assistance has for some time been available for subsequent visits on the same basis as for convicted prisoners. Since 1 April 1991, the scheme has been extended to cover visits to convicted prisoners serving sentences of less than three months. Further extensions will be considered as resources permit;

▶ **extending the availability of cardphones.** Cardphones will be provided in all those establishments which do not already have them;

▶ **abolishing the routine reading of letters in all establishments, except dispersal prisons.** Incoming mail is still searched for contraband such as drugs, while Governors retain the right, and may be required, to read an individual's mail for security reasons;

▶ **increasing home leave.** The opportunities for home leave in open prisons have been increased from three times a year to six times a year.

7.37 The Prison Service will continue to look for ways of improving opportunities for prisoners to maintain links with their families, subject to resource and staffing implications, and to the necessary security requirements. In particular, the Prison Service will:

▶ **consider the further extension of home leave arrangements,** including for prisoners in prisons located away from their home areas;

▶ **consider the scope for increasing the length and informality of visits from particular members of the family.** In the first instance, it will consider extending the scheme at Holloway prison which provides for day visits by children to their mothers, initially to other women's prisons and, subject to experience, to selected male prisons. In the light of its review of home leave arrangements, it will consider the feasibility and desirability of private family visits for certain prisoners, particularly those who, because of their location or circumstances, are near the end of their sentences but not eligible for home leave;

▶ **encourage the appointment of more Prison Visitors** – volunteers from the community who visit prisoners who may not otherwise receive visits – and consider the scope for increasing the involvement of voluntary support groups with prisoners and their families;

▶ **increase the number of places in mother and baby units.** A new unit for nine mothers and their babies will be opened at New Hall prison in 1993/94. The Prison Service will consider whether further places are required;

▶ **continue to provide improved visiting facilities** in the course of its new building and prison refurbishment programmes;

▶ **consider ways of increasing the provision of visitors' centres** where prisoners' families can wait before the start of the visit and can receive advice and assistance from local voluntary bodies;

▶ **encourage Governors to make provision for creches** for the young children of visitors where space and resources permit.

Particular Requirements

7.38 The Prison Service is likely in future to be holding a larger proportion of prisoners who have committed particularly serious offences involving violence and sexual deviance. Their behaviour may have been exacerbated by drug and alcohol misuse. Some of these prisoners might be able to avoid reoffending if they could be helped to understand what they have done, what its consequences have been and how to avoid repeating such behaviour in future.

7.39 The Prison Service will also continue to hold prisoners suffering from acute physical or mental incapacities. It must improve the effectiveness of its provision for them.

7.40 The Prison Service intends to develop particular programmes for the following groups of offenders:

▶ **sex offenders.** Programmes will be introduced from this year to tackle sex offenders' distorted beliefs about their relationships, to make them more aware of the effect of their offences on the victim, and to ensure these prisoners take responsibility for and face up to the consequences of their behaviour. Priority in the programmes will be given to those likely to present the greatest risk on release. Prisoners sentenced for sexual offences will be assessed following reception. Two main programmes will be available: a core programme which will challenge attitudes and teach prisoners how to control their behaviour and to avoid high risk situations; and an extended programme with more specialist provision. They will be rigorously evaluated. The programmes will be multi-disciplinary, including prison officers, probation and education staff. They will lay the foundations for the work that will need to be continued after the prisoner's release under the extended supervision arrangements for sex offenders in the Criminal Justice Act 1991;

▶ **drug and alcohol misusers.** Drug and alcohol misuse are significant factors in the lives and often the offences of many prisoners. The Prison Service plans to develop and refine its programmes to assist prisoners in overcoming such misuse and to encourage them to seek treatment. It will encourage establishments to work closely with voluntary and other agencies in preparing such prisoners for release. The programmes will draw on existing experience with counselling and group work. The Prison Service will consider also the experience of prison systems which have introduced special drug units for prisoners who wish to receive help and have their progress monitored. Revised guidelines on the care of drug misusers were issued in April 1991. These guidelines gave advice on medical aspects, including the use of substitute drugs during withdrawal; on the provision of continuing support, particularly from probation officers; on drawing on assistance from approved agencies in the community; and on the appointment of key functional managers in prisons to develop and co-ordinate services. A resource manual for staff was issued in May 1991 to complement these guidelines;

▶ **violent offenders.** The Prison Service intends to draw on experience of the programmes for sex offenders to develop additional modules which will address the behaviour of those who find it particularly difficult to control their anger.

7.41 The Prison Service will also consider extending its work on programmes which provide for prisoners with special health care and related needs. In particular:

▶ **HIV/AIDS.** The Prison Service aims to prevent prisoners becoming infected and to prevent the transmission of infection to others. It is committed to assisting those who may have been at risk of acquiring HIV infection. It aims to provide as normal a life in prison as possible for HIV infected prisoners who are well, and appropriate care in prison and (when

necessary) in outside hospitals and hospices for those who become ill. The Government accepts the Woolf Report's proposal that there should be a thorough review of present policies. The review will examine the best ways of achieving the objectives outlined above. It will include an examination of the system of viral infectivity restrictions introduced in 1985, possible options for reducing the risk of infection and the contribution which research might be able to make. The review's recommendations will be considered as they become available over the course of the next year. In the meantime, a revised statement of Prison Service policy and operating guidelines will be issued reflecting the main proposals on the management of HIV/AIDS in the Woolf Report. Since 1985 the Prison Service has made information available to prisoners and staff, has set up staff training programmes and has provided guidance to Governors and managing medical officers on best practice. Clinical guidelines issued to medical officers in May 1990 emphasised the importance of a multi-disciplinary approach. This approach is reflected in a new training course and associated working manual for operational and specialist managers introduced this year;

▶ **mental disorder and physical illness.** Mentally disordered and disturbed prisoners must be looked after with special care. Those who meet the statutory criteria for transfer to hospital for treatment should be moved to suitable health service facilities as soon as possible. There are also other prisoners who have long-term, but not terminal, illnesses who do not require or who cannot for security reasons be given hospital treatment in the outside community. Such prisoners may be able to be accommodated within normal living units with other prisoners, at least for some part of their sentences, if particular care is given to their allocation and their programme. Others, for at least some part of their time in prison, will need more specialist care and attention. At present, such prisoners may be allocated to a prison hospital. The Prison Service will consider the case for establishing a small number of special care centres in selected prisons which would specialise in the care of such prisoners.

Suicide and Self-Harm

7.42 The Prison Service has undertaken a fundamental review of its response to the problem of suicide and self-harm in the light of the Report by Her Majesty's Chief Inspector of Prisons (4). The Government agrees with the Chief Inspector's view that there is no one simple answer to the problem, and that it requires a broad approach to improving the conditions and treatment of all prisoners.

7.43 There has been considerable public concern, and distress within the Prison Service, about the numbers of suicides by prisoners in recent years. A suicide causes deep and understandable grief to the victim's family. It creates stress and concern to other prisoners, to the staff involved and to their families. Given the pressures of imprisonment, and the nature of the prison population, it is inevitable that many prisoners will at some time experience anxiety and depression. Experience in prisons and other residential institutions around the world, and in the community, has shown that it is often very difficult to identify the moments of

greatest crisis. Practical arrangements for protecting those who are known to be at risk from harming themselves have to be balanced with the importance of creating an environment in which prisoners can retain some degree of personal responsibility and choice. Not every suicide can be prevented, but many prisoners can be helped through periods of despair.

7.44 Specific measures for the prevention of suicide and self-harm are not alone sufficient. They must be provided against a range of wider measures which together help to reduce the likelihood of such incidents occurring. It is particularly important that relationships in prisons are such that prisoners who may be feeling suicidal can get the help and support they need, from prison staff, from their families, from outside agencies or from other prisoners.

7.45 The Chief Inspector's wide-ranging approach to reducing the risk of suicide and self-harm is reflected in many parts of this White Paper. Of particular relevance are the Government's proposals for:

▶ improving arrangements for supporting prison staff following incidents (Chapter 2);

▶ the treatment and care of all prisoners by staff (Chapter 4);

▶ reviewing the training of prison staff (Chapter 4);

▶ providing decent physical conditions, particularly access to sanitation (Chapter 6);

▶ reducing overcrowding (Chapter 6);

▶ developing a code of standards (Chapter 6);

▶ providing a high quality of health care (Chapter 6);

▶ developing active programmes for prisoners (Chapter 7);

▶ reviewing arrangements for the reception and induction of prisoners (Chapter 7);

▶ extending personal officer schemes (Chapter 7);

▶ enabling prisoners to maintain their family links (Chapter 7).

7.46 The Prison Service has also reviewed its specific arrangements for suicide prevention in the light of the recommendations in the Chief Inspector's Report, which it very largely accepts. Thorough local reviews have been carried out by Suicide Prevention Management Groups in accordance with new guidance issued in December 1990. The Prison Service aims to ensure that a high level of awareness is maintained in the future and that it builds on the efforts already being made by Governors and their staff to prevent suicides. In particular, the Prison Service will:

▶ **send a further supportive message to all staff from the Director of Inmate Administration.** The message will recognise the stress which suicides cause. It will encourage close co-operation between staff. It will reinforce the value of the work of each establishment's Suicide Prevention Management Group;

▶ **continue to encourage the work of the**

Samaritans in prisons. Over 80 establishments already have links with Samaritan branches. New guidelines will be issued on access to the Samaritans through visits, letters and phone calls;

▶ **prepare with the Samaritans a training video for staff** on the care of prisoners and the prevention of suicide;

▶ **arrange in October and November of this year training days** for governor grades, doctors, hospital officers and suicide prevention trainers;

▶ **carry out pilot schemes in which selected prisoners would assist in suicide prevention** by attending the Suicide Prevention Management Group and by being trained to be aware of, and support, other prisoners who are at risk;

▶ **introduce a trial of in-cell closed circuit television** as an aid to keeping under supportive observation prisoners presenting a high risk of suicide;

▶ **review the potential suicide risk in the design of cells,** in particular cell windows;

▶ **review arrangements for access to cells in emergencies during the night;**

▶ **review the guidance issued to establishments following the results of research into attempted suicide and self-harm in prison establishments.** This research is being carried out for the Prison Service by the University of Cambridge. It will be completed in the spring of 1992.

Conclusion

7.47 The Prison Service's task is to look after prisoners. All other aspects of its work are designed to help meet this objective by creating the circumstances in which effective programmes can be provided in sufficiently secure surroundings at a reasonable cost. The proposals in this Chapter should not, therefore, be seen in isolation. The creation of a fully active and demanding day for prisoners relevant to their circumstances and located reasonably close to their homes and families will depend on achieving the management and staffing structures, and the smaller living units in community prisons, which have been described earlier in this White Paper. It is within such an environment that staff are most likely to establish the constructive and caring relationships with prisoners on which these programmes depend.

Notes

(1) "Women and Prison", Report of an ad-hoc Working Group of the Women's National Commission, Cabinet Office, April 1991.

(2) BS 5750 is an accredited standard of the British Standards Institution specifying production and management systems which ensure that products or services meet the quality required by the customer.

(3) The National Prison Survey was conducted by the Office of Population Censuses and Surveys between January and March 1991. It was commissioned on behalf of the Prison Service by the Home Office Research and Planning Unit. The analysis of its results will be completed later this year.

(4) "Report of a Review by Her Majesty's Chief Inspector of Prisons for England and Wales of Suicide and Self- harm in Prison Service Establishments in England and Wales", HMSO, December 1990 (Cm 1383).

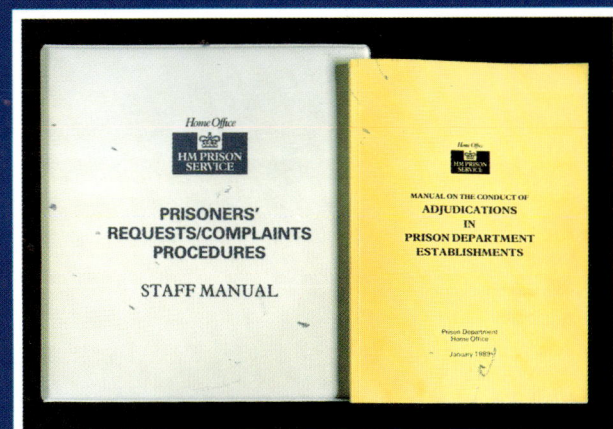

Chapter 8

1

3

2

1 Prison Service manuals

2 Prisoner with request/complaint form – HMP Durham

3 A typical Governor's adjudication – HMP Winchester

4

4 Prisoner in
discussion with a
member of the
Board of Visitors –
HMP Brixton

5 Area Manager
considering a
prisoner's
complaint –
Prison Service HQ,
London

5

Introduction

8.1   All institutions and communities require a system through which an individual's grievances or concerns can be considered and resolved. All institutions and communities equally require means of enforcing their rules and procedures and effective sanctions for those who disobey.

8.2   There is an obligation on the Prison Service to ensure that the standards to which it operates are consistent with the standards expected of any part of the criminal justice system. The rules must be fair and just, known to everyone concerned and followed in accordance with accepted and fair procedures. The procedures must provide opportunities for conflicts to be resolved quickly so that the daily life of the community is not disrupted. Prisoners must feel that there are effective ways of having their complaints heard and redressed. Management must ensure that informal disciplinary systems are not allowed to develop. The procedures must command the confidence of everyone in the prison.

Existing Provisions

8.3   The Prison Service introduced a new complaints procedure in September 1990 following an extensive review and widespread consultation. The new system encourages problems to be resolved informally wherever possible; but provides a formal structure to which every prisoner has a right of access. The formal structure allows complaints to be considered at increasingly senior levels within set time limits, and ensures that the reasons for decisions are given in writing. The system continues to allow prisoners at any time to take up their points of concern with people outside prison management – including Boards of Visitors, the European Court of Human Rights in Strasbourg, his or her Member of Parliament, and, through the Member of Parliament, with the Parliamentary Commissioner for Administration. The system does not provide, however, for access to a complaints Commissioner, unless the prisoner alleges maladministration. When it introduced the new complaints system, the Government gave a commitment to consider the appointment of a prisons Ombudsman in the light of experience of the operation of the new system.

8.4   The present disciplinary procedures in the Prison Service have also been extensively reviewed, most recently in 1985 by the Prior Committee (1). A series of improvements have been made since then. They include:

▶   a complete revision of the code of offences, to make the Rules clearer and simpler;

▶   a reduction in the maximum punishment available to Boards of Visitors (from 180 to 120 days loss of remission for adults and 120 to 90 days loss of remission for young prisoners, on a single offence);

▶   the abolition of the offences of making a false and malicious allegation against an officer and of repeatedly making groundless complaints;

▶   the revision and publication of the manual on the Conduct of Adjudications and the associated Standing Order (3D);

▶   improved training for Governors and Boards of Visitors in conducting adjudications;

▶   revised instructions issued in June 1991

on the restoration of lost remission. These provide for a reduction in the qualifying period before restoration of remission may be considered. They emphasise the importance of the prisoner being able to show constructive behaviour since the offence and provide that the prisoner will be given written reasons for the Governor's or the Board of Visitors' decision.

8.5   In 1987 the Government decided not to implement the Prior Committee's central proposal – to replace the Boards of Visitors' work in considering disciplinary offences with a series of tribunals under a legally qualified President. Instead the Prison Service introduced an experiment involving the use of Magistrates' Clerks to assist some 13 Boards of Visitors during their disciplinary hearings. The Government has considered the matter further, in the light of the assessment of the experiment (2), the recommendations of the Woolf Report and the subsequent consultation paper issued by the Prison Service (3).

General Principles

8.6   Many of the proposals in this White Paper are directed to improving relations between prisoners and staff in prisons. They include the prisoner's "compact", involving prisoners in sentence planning, giving reasons for decisions, improving physical conditions and providing more active programmes. They include also the proposal to create better jobs for staff. Together they should help to improve the way day to day relations in prisons are conducted and so bring down the volume and seriousness of complaints and the incidence of disciplinary offences. Procedures for complaints and discipline should underpin the day to day

conduct of relations in a prison – they should not constitute the primary channel through which these relations are conducted.

8.7   The following general principles should apply to procedures relating both to complaints and to discipline:

▷   the systems should ensure that all involved in them are treated fairly, with justice and respect; and should ensure that all relevant representations are heard and responded to;

▷   the procedures and safeguards should be proportionate to the seriousness of the offence or the complaint;

▷   the systems should enable problems to be resolved quickly;

▷   the systems should allow problems to be resolved at the lowest level practicable;

▷   procedures should be as simple and as straightforward as possible;

▷   there should be an avenue of appeal against decisions, ultimately to a body independent of the Prison Service.

Future Direction

8.8   In the light of these principles, the Government intends to extend and revise the procedures as follows:

▶   **Governors should conduct all disciplinary cases within their current powers** – the maximum penalty would therefore be 28 days loss of remission or, once the relevant provision of the Criminal Justice Act 1991 is implemented, 28 added days. Charges should no longer be referred to Boards of Visitors able to deploy more severe powers of punishment;

▶ **serious criminal offences committed in prison should be referred to the police for investigation** with a view to possible prosecution in the courts by the Crown Prosecution Service;

▶ **prisoners should be able to appeal against the disciplinary decisions of the Governor to the Area Manager.** The Area Manager should be able to review the Governor's decision and the procedures followed. Further consideration will be given to whether Area Managers should be enabled to rehear cases, taking account of the implications for their workload and other responsibilities;

▶ **there should be an independent avenue of appeal against a disciplinary finding once avenues within the Prison Service have been exhausted.** The full implementation of this proposal is likely to require primary legislation. Further consideration will need to be given in advance of such legislation to the nature of the appellate body, and to its powers and procedures. The Government is attracted, however, to the notion of a Complaints Adjudicator broadly on the lines recommended in the Woolf Report;

▶ **appeals against decisions made in response to complaints should also be able to be considered by the same independent body.** Consideration will need to be given to the scope and powers of the body in receiving and considering complaints. There may be some areas which it would not be appropriate to refer to such a body. In particular, it would not consider appeals against parole decisions;

▶ **prisoners would continue to be able to exercise their existing rights of access to outside bodies and complaints mechanisms,** including to Members of Parliament and, through them, to the Parliamentary Commissioner for Administration.

8.9 These proposals represent a significant change in the way disciplinary proceedings are to be handled. The procedure will in future be more closely akin to the system in Scotland where disciplinary matters and offences in prison are dealt with either by the Governor or by the courts. It would, in addition, provide for an independent avenue of appeal from the Governor's decision once the matter had been considered by the Area Manager.

8.10 The proposals for the handling of complaints would build on the arrangements already in place. They were described earlier in this Chapter. They were generally welcomed by the Woolf Report. They will continue to provide for the informal and formal resolution of problems, with scope for appeal up the management chain and access to the Board of Visitors at any time. The arrangements for prisoners to write in confidence to the Governor, Area Manager or Chairman of the Board of Visitors will in future make clear to the prisoner that complaints against staff will be shown to the staff concerned, as the Woolf Report proposed. The independent appeal body would be a final avenue of appeal on top of the existing grievance arrangements.

Boards of Visitors

8.11 It is a consequence of these proposals that Boards of Visitors will no longer exercise an adjudicatory role. The Government pays tribute to the care and diligence which Boards of Visitors have shown in carrying out this work over many years. This decision is no reflection on the quality of their individual or collective contributions. But the Government recognises, as many members of Boards of Visitors themselves have recognised, that the Board's ability to conduct its central watch-dog role has been hampered by its work on adjudications.

8.12 To undertake its watch-dog role effectively, the Board of Visitors must command the confidence of prisoners. The Government accepts that confidence will be increased if prisoners do not see members of Boards of Visitors as people who are responsible for imposing disciplinary punishments. The Government accepts also that the hearing of charges against a prisoner which constitute a serious criminal offence should be subject to the normal safeguards and procedures of the criminal law.

8.13 The implementation of this decision should not, in the Government's view, be dependent on the legislation to appoint an independent complaints body. It will, however, require a revision of the Prison Rules and some administrative preparations in prisons and with the police and prosecuting authorities. These preparations will be taken forward as quickly as possible. In the meantime, Boards of Visitors will be asked to continue to hear disciplinary cases under their present powers.

8.14 Once this decision has been implemented, the central role of the Boards of Visitors should be enhanced and strengthened.

Members of Boards need to be fully effective and independent monitors of the establishment to which they are appointed. They have the right, if necessary, of direct access to the Secretary of State and are able to publish their views and their annual reports. Because they have access to the prison at any time, they provide protection for both prisoners and staff, and for the reputation and standing of the Prison Service as a whole.

8.15 The Government looks to the Boards of Visitors, therefore, to develop their work as the watch-dogs of the system. In particular, and among their other duties, they will continue:

▶ to authorise removal from association for vulnerable prisoners under the present Rule 43;

▶ to authorise removal from association under Rule 43 in the interests of good order or discipline – this function is best performed by Boards of Visitors rather than by headquarters Area Managers (as proposed in the Woolf Report) since Area Managers cannot be expected always to be in a position to visit the prisoner at the time or shortly after sanctioning the prisoner's continued removal from association. The Board of Visitors is best placed to satisfy itself that it is necessary for segregation to continue;

▶ to advise and assist prisoners who have concerns and grievances, including providing them with any necessary assistance in taking the matter through the grievance procedure. Boards will be able to monitor the conduct of the disciplinary system and satisfy themselves that both prisoners and staff are properly protected;

▶ to monitor closely the treatment of prisoners and their access to facilities;

▶ to monitor closely the administration of all areas of the establishment.

8.16 Boards should know clearly the nature of their duties and their powers and responsibilities. There is benefit in spreading good ideas and examples of sound practice between Boards. Much of this can be achieved by individual Boards in briefing new members and through conferences and the work of the Boards of Visitors Co-ordinating Committee. But the Prison Service also has a part to play. It provided Boards of Visitors in August this year with a new manual setting out the roles and responsibilities of members and the procedures they should follow. For the future, the Prison Service intends:

▶ **to enhance the training offered to members of Boards of Visitors.** This training will take account of the comments on Boards of Visitors which were made in the Woolf Report;

▶ **to examine ways of providing better administrative and other support for Boards** – the overall budget for travelling and subsistence and other expenses has been increased by 20% for the current financial year.

8.17 The work of Boards is a demanding public service requiring people of high integrity and commitment. The Prison Service and the public have been well served by Boards of Visitors over many years, as the Woolf Report confirmed. The continued quality of their contribution depends on attracting members from all parts of the community, including members of the ethnic minorities. The Government intends to continue to develop ways of encouraging a wider membership of Boards of Visitors. The Government will also consider whether this objective and the work of the Boards of Visitors are likely to be assisted by the appointment of a President, as proposed in the Woolf Report.

Conclusion

8.18 The proposals set out in this Chapter should ensure that there are well-founded procedures for resolving complaints and disciplinary offences which are fair, just and proportionate; and they should contribute to more confident and harmonious relations within prison establishments. They will reinforce the independent role of the Board of Visitors in monitoring the day to day life of the prison and will provide a separate independent appeal body at the apex of the formal procedures. As a result, the quality of relationships in establishments should be improved, and the right standards of justice maintained.

Notes

(1) "Report of the Committee on the Prison Disciplinary System", HMSO, October 1985 (Cmnd 9641-I,II).

(2) "Qualified Clerks at Boards of Visitors' Disciplinary Hearings: Report of an Experiment in 13 Prisons" by Helen Jones and Rod Morgan, University of Bristol, published by the Home Office, December 1990.

(3) "The Prison Disciplinary System – consultation document on Lord Justice Woolf's proposal that Boards of Visitors should cease to conduct adjudications", issued March 1991.

1 Prison officer and probation officer giving prisoner bail advice – HMP Winchester

2 New bail hostel – Northumbria Probation Service

3

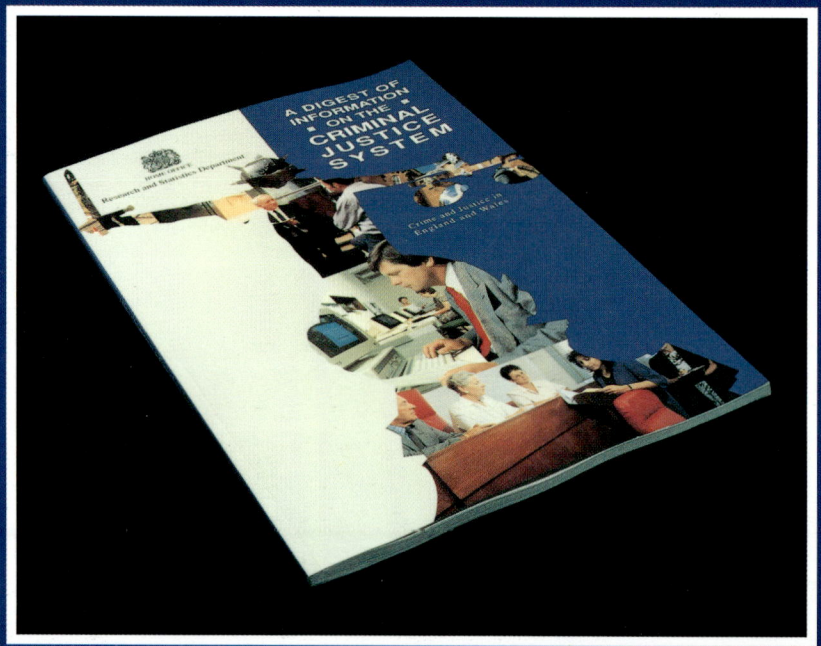

3 Employment assessment project available to prisoners on temporary release – Nottinghamshire Probation Service.

4 Home Office Digest of Information on the Criminal Justice System – published in March 1991

4

Introduction

9.1 The Prison Service can provide a fully effective service only if it maintains close links with other parts of the criminal justice system. It provides services for and receives services from other agencies and institutions and, like any provider of services, has to keep in touch with those on whom it relies. There needs, therefore, to be close relations at local level between prison establishments and the police service; the Crown Prosecution Service; the probation service; the personal social services; the education services; hospitals and the courts. The Prison Service must also seek to meet the needs of defence lawyers who wish to have access to their clients in custody. It must maintain close links with voluntary organisations.

9.2 The Government has accepted the case for additional structures at both area and national levels to help in focusing the necessary co-operation, co-ordination and exchange of information. This is described in Chapter 1. But the Government is committed also to further specific steps in developing links between the Prison Service and the probation service; and in carrying forward its declared policy that imprisonment should be used only for those who must be held in this way. These steps are described in this Chapter.

Relations with the Probation Service

9.3 The Government recognises the value of developing close relations between the Prison Service and the probation service. The probation service must know about and contribute to the Prison Service's work if it is to be able effectively to take up the reins of supervision following the prisoner's release from custody. The Government announced in its decision document on the probation service

(1) that it supported the principle of close co-operation between the two services and would consider with both services how best to ensure that is effected. This will include considering whether a professional probation presence in Prison Service Headquarters would be helpful.

9.4 In addition, the Government will:

▶ **enshrine the need for co-operation between the probation service and the Prison Service in national standards for the supervision of offenders by the probation service.** The standards will establish the procedures necessary to provide continuity between the part of the offender's sentence in custody and the part in the community. They will require that probation service supervision programmes are developed with the close co-operation of prison officers, probation officers seconded to prisons and probation officers from the prisoner's home area;

▶ **issue new guidance this October on throughcare and the role of probation officers in prisons.** This will reflect the strengthened relationship required under the Criminal Justice Act 1991. It will enhance the work of probation officers by encouraging the full use of their social work skills. The guidance will encourage feedback from the home probation area to the relevant prison at the end of the period of supervision so that the effectiveness of prison programmes can be assessed;

▶ **introduce management contracts between the Governor of each establishment and the relevant chief**

probation officer. These contracts will govern the work of the probation service in relation to that establishment. They will draw on the experience of operating such contracts in, for example, Erlestoke and Risley prisons;

▶ **encourage probation officers working in prisons to be involved in the preparation of sentence plans for prisoners** (these are described in Chapter 7);

▶ **introduce as resources allow opportunities for joint training** involving prison staff and the probation service. The organisation of this training will take account of the Report of the Efficiency Scrutiny of In-Service Probation Training which was published in May 1991 (2).

Bail Schemes

9.5   The Government supports the development of bail information schemes in magistrates' courts. They are a valuable way of ensuring that the Crown Prosecution Service has the information on which to base recommendations about remands, and, in turn, that magistrates can make an informed decision about granting bail within the terms of the Bail Act 1976. The probation service is currently providing information to the Crown Prosecution Service in 103 magistrates' courts in England and Wales.

9.6   The Government supports also the extension of bail information schemes to those prisons which hold prisoners on remand. There are bail information schemes available in eight prisons at present. Such schemes, often involving probation officers working closely with prison officers, can help to provide information which on a second or subsequent appearance will assist the Crown Prosecution Service and hence the courts in determining whether continued remands in custody are necessary. They complement the existing work of prison officers in bail units or acting as bail officers in local prisons and remand centres, who help prisoners with their bail applications. Probation and prison officers attend the same national training courses on bail information work.

9.7   Approved bail hostels are a valuable way of providing closely supervised accommodation for those whom the courts might otherwise remand in custody. The Government's programme is designed to provide 1,200 new places at approved hostels between 1988 and 1994. More than 400 of these places have already been provided and many more will soon become available. The Government seeks to encourage the provision of sufficient accommodation outside the approved sector for those who do not require close supervision. The Government wishes also to encourage the development of specialist bail accommodation and supervision for those who appear to be mentally disturbed, or who have problems with drug or alcohol misuse. In these ways, the Government wishes to see a range of hostel accommodation provided with different levels of supervision.

9.8   In taking forward these objectives, the Government will:

▶ **extend bail information schemes to all probation areas as resources allow;**

▶ **extend bail information schemes to about eight other prisons by the end** of 1991/92 and subsequently to all local and remand prisons as resources allow;

▶ improve the availability of bail beds in the independent sector, beginning in April 1992;

▶ consider further the balance of provision required for mentally disordered and substance misusers at existing approved hostels, new specialist approved hostels and places outside the approved sector.

Mentally Disordered Offenders

9.9 Prison is not a suitable place for people suffering from serious mental disturbance. Whenever possible, such offenders should be diverted to the health or social services when they first come into contact with the criminal justice system. Where it is unavoidable that those requiring in-patient treatment are committed to prison, then they should be transferred to suitable health service facilities as soon as possible.

9.10 These principles were confirmed by the Government following an Inter-Departmental Working Group on mentally disturbed offenders in prison in England and Wales which reported in May 1987. In particular, the Government has:

issued to the courts in July 1990 a new edition of the Home Office booklet "The Sentence of the Court" with a substantially revised chapter on mentally disordered offenders. The chapter emphasises the desirability of courts using their statutory powers to remand particularly disordered defendants to

hospital for assessment or treatment;

issued a Home Office circular in September 1990 to the police, courts and others in the criminal justice system. The circular emphasised the importance of the prompt identification and assessment of offenders suspected of suffering from mental disorder and the need to consider at each stage the possibility of diversion from the criminal justice system. It set out examples of good working practice, including the psychiatric assessment services at Bow Street, Marlborough Street and Horseferry Road magistrates' courts and the duty psychiatrist scheme at Peterborough magistrates' court;

issued through the Department of Health a copy of the Home Office circular to all health and social services authorities, with a letter drawing attention to their responsibilities for ensuring that sufficient facilities are available for mentally disordered offenders;

included in the Criminal Justice Act 1991 measures to help the courts to deal appropriately with mentally disordered offenders. Once the provisions are implemented, courts will be able to require local social services authorities to provide information to assist them in deciding whether to make guardianship orders in respect of convicted mentally disordered offenders. Courts will be required to consider any information available to them about a person's mental condition before imposing a custodial sentence and must take account of the effect of such a sentence on his or her condition and its treatment;

▶ provided some £315,000 over three years to fund the National Association for the Care and Resettlement of Offenders to provide two pilot projects in Merseyside and West Yorkshire aimed at encouraging greater co-operation in diverting mentally disordered persons from the criminal justice system or in arranging for alternatives to remanding them in custody. These projects began in July 1990. Once completed, they will be evaluated by the Home Office, along with a similar NACRO project in the West Midlands, to measure their impact and the resource implications of any extension;

▶ provided nearly £100,000 over two years to the Hertfordshire Care Trust to promote and develop the use of psychiatric assessment panels initiated in North West Hertfordshire as a means of diverting mentally disordered persons from the criminal justice system. This scheme too will be evaluated by the Home Office.

9.11 The Government also established at the end of 1990 a joint Department of Health/Home Office review. The Committee steering the review includes representatives of both Departments, the health and social services and the criminal justice agencies. Its purpose is to review the level, pattern and operation of health and social services for mentally disordered offenders. This includes the present arrangements for funding developments and ways of improving them. The review is considering also the level of psychiatric services required in prison and their relationship with the services provided by the Special Hospitals Service Authority and the National Health Service. It will consider the case for a further

prison providing therapeutic regimes on the lines of Grendon Underwood prison. The review is due to be completed in mid-1992. The Steering Committee is required to submit regular progress reports to Ministers. These reports will allow any necessary early action to be taken.

9.12 Taken together, this represents a substantial programme to improve the provision for mentally disordered offenders and the arrangements for diverting them from custody. The Government will consider in the light of the review's findings and recommendations what further steps may be necessary to ensure that mentally disordered offenders are not unnecessarily held in prison.

Information to the Sentencing Court

9.13 Sentencing courts should have available information about prisons in their areas, and the facilities which they provide. It is not the job of sentencers to take decisions about the allocation to a particular prison of those remanded in custody or to take into account in their sentencing the conditions in any particular establishment. But the Government accepts that courts may wish to have as full information as possible about prisons and imprisonment. They should also be aware of the costs of imprisonment and other sentences.

9.14 To these ends, the Government will:

▶ **publish each year information to enable courts and others to be aware of the financial implications of their decisions, and to help them carry out their duty not to discriminate on grounds of race or sex,** in accordance with the provisions in Section 95 of the Criminal Justice Act 1991;

▶ **make available to the courts information about local sentencing patterns** on the lines of information provided to magistrates' courts between May and July 1991, in conjunction with the Magistrates' Association and the Justices' Clerks Society;

▶ **provide through the Prison Service to individual courts information about the prisons in their catchment areas.**

Conclusion

9.15 The effects of these proposals will be to improve the quality of information available in the criminal justice system, to provide better arrangements in the community for offenders and for those charged with offences, and to develop closer links between the Prison and probation services.

Notes

(1) "Organising Supervision & Punishment in the Community", Decision Document, Home Office, April 1991.

(2) "Report of a Scrutiny of Probation In-Service Training", by S Hadjipavlou, S C Murphy and G A Green, Home Office, May 1991.

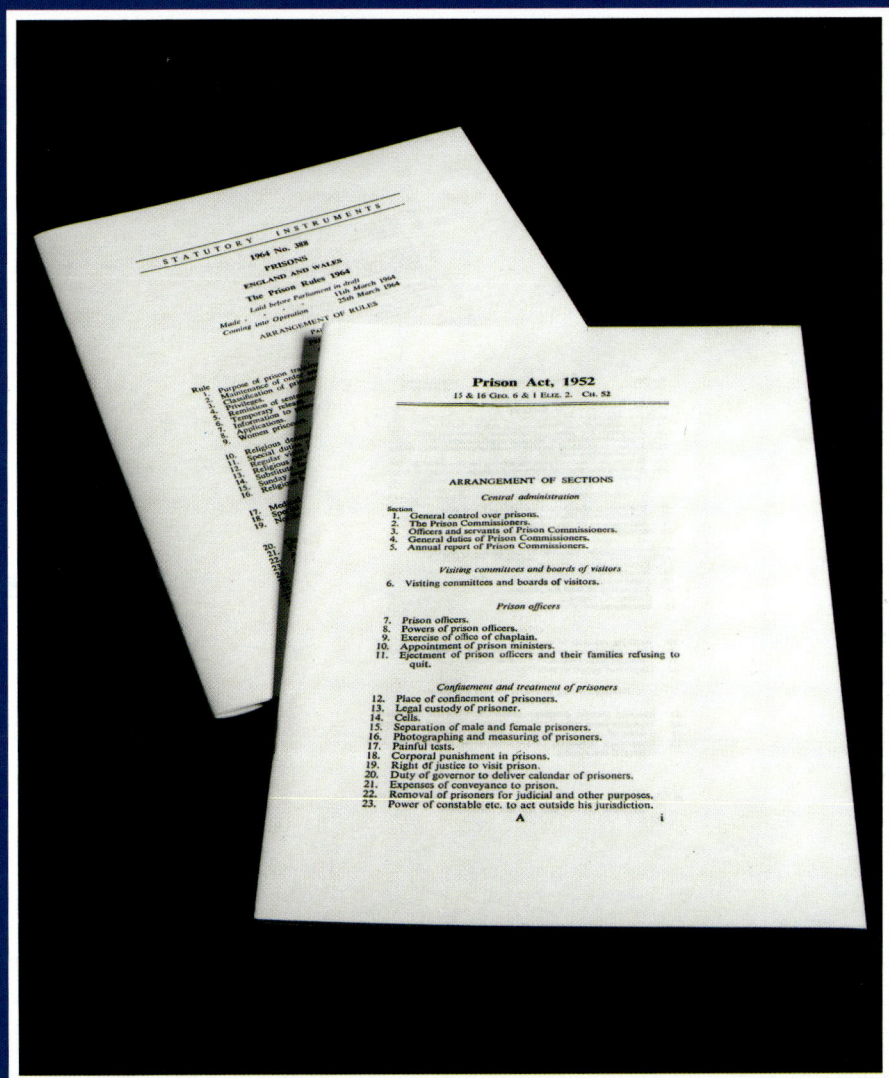

Introduction

10.1 The Prison Service is governed by the Prison Act 1952. The statutory framework for the Prison Service is now almost 40 years old. Much of that Act repeated earlier legislation; some from the 19th century.

10.2 The Prison Rules date from 1964. Many have since been revised, and others have been added. But the structure is now over 25 years old. There has been no comprehensive revision or consolidation of the Rules since then.

A New Prison Act and New Prison Rules

10.3 The actions identified in this White Paper do not, for the most part, depend on primary legislation. Only the appointment of an independent body to hear and determine disciplinary appeals is likely to need such legislation.

10.4 A number of the proposals in this White Paper will require amendments to the Rules. They include:

▶ separate rules for unconvicted prisoners on remand;

▶ changes in visits entitlements;

▶ removal of the adjudicatory role of Boards of Visitors;

▶ the provision for vulnerable prisoners.

10.5 The necessary revisions or additions to the Prison Rules will be made as they are required.

10.6 The Government considers, however, that in due course a more fundamental revision of the statutory framework for the Prison Service would be desirable. The legislation should reflect the outcome of many of the major developments identified in this White Paper. Examples might be:

▶ establishing in legislation the duties of the Prison Service;

▶ establishing a domestic legislative basis for the treatment of unconvicted prisoners;

▶ putting Boards of Visitors on a fresh statutory basis;

▶ providing for the Prison Service's code of standards;

▶ providing a statutory framework for an independent appeal body.

10.7 Much further work is required on many of these developments before a decision can be made about their inclusion in legislation and the form such legislation might take. Some developments will need to be piloted so that their effectiveness can be assessed.

10.8 Subject to the passage of the legislation, it would be desirable to review, reformulate and consolidate the Prison Rules to provide an up-to-date statement of what is required of the Prison Service.

Conclusion

10.9 The introduction of new legislation at the right time will provide an opportunity for Parliament to consider the statutory framework for the Prison Service, the powers which it requires and what is expected of it. The Government believes that such legislation is necessary to provide a modern structure, approved by Parliament, to take the Prison Service forward into the next century. This legislation should firmly establish the Prison Service as a body providing a service necessary to the public and of value to the prisoners in its care.

Printed in the United Kingdom for HMSO.
Dd 0506962 9/91. C75 51 8242 O/N 166057.